a time to Pray

Readings and Prayers for Daily Life & Worship

Richard Garrard

Kevin
Mayhew

First published in 1993 by
KEVIN MAYHEW LTD
Rattlesden
Bury St Edmunds
Suffolk IP30 0SZ

© 1993 Kevin Mayhew Ltd

ISBN   0 86209 398 8

Front cover: *The Annuciation* by Pickford Marriot.
Reproduced by kind permission of
Fine Art Photographic Library Ltd, London.

Cover design by Graham Johnstone
Typesetting and Page Creation by Anne Haskell
Printed and bound in Great Britain.

CONTENTS

CONTENTS

ACKNOWLEDGEMENTS

In providing Bible and Psalm readings throughout this book the author has drawn upon several publications. The publishers wish to thank the following for permission to reproduce these readings:

T.E.V. (Today's English Version – The Good News Bible), 1976. Reproduced by permission of the Bible Society, Stonehill Green, Westlea, Swindon SN5 7OG.

R.E.B. (Revised English Bible), copyright 1989, Oxford and Cambridge University Presses. Reproduced by permission.

J.B. (The Jerusalem Bible), published (and copyright) 1966, 1967 and 1968, by Darton Longman & Todd Ltd., and Doubleday & Co Inc., and used by permission of the publishers.

R.S.V. (Revised Standard Version), copyright 1946, 1952 and 1971 by the Division of Christian Education of the National Council of Churches of Christ in the USA, and used by permission.

A.S.B. (Alternative Service Book). From the Liturgical Psalter. Reproduced by permission of Harper-Collins Publishers, London.

Unless stated, all Psalm extracts are from A.S.B. In every other case the Bible version used is indicated after chapter and verse.

Every effort has been made to trace the owners of copyright material, and we hope that no copyright has been infringed. Pardon is sought and apology is made if the contrary be the case, and a correction will be made in any reprint of this book.

ABOUT THIS BOOK

The simple aim of this collection of readings and prayers is to help you to pray with imagination and interest.

This is not a book about prayer but a series of orders of prayer which you are invited to use as laid out or adapt as you find most helpful. The method is to put Bible readings beside non-biblical material to stimulate thought and prayer, offering new insights, new angles of vision, new ways of getting God in focus.

Each 'order of service' has within it the formula:

PICTURE • PONDER • PRAY • PROMISE

These words are an invitation to let your mind run on the readings so that ideas, vision, prayers and resolutions can result. Be adventurous, think wide, but always seek to return in thought and prayer to the God who is life and whose love for us never fails. Bring him thanks, sorrow and requests – let your imagination be set on fire.

Each 'order' is designed to be used by two or more people, but they can just as well be used on your own, in a quiet place, or a railway train, in the morning or evening or whenever you can find time to pray.

If used by a group, then the **PICTURE • PONDER • PRAY • PROMISE** selection can encourage a time for shared prayer, opportunities for prayer in one's own words, pointers for further investigation, starting-points for discussion. Equally it can help to encourage a time of silence for each person to use as they wish.

If used alone, then a note-book or any scrap of paper can help the praying process by brief notes, jottings or pictures to engage and use all our faculties in focusing on God – Creator, Saviour, Spirit.

Two warnings go with this book:

Do not strain to be super-holy. Let the words and images flow over you. You can always come back to a section at some later time, and you are likely to find that the second time round will yield new thoughts, pictures and prayers quite different from those which came to you during your previous readings. This is all to the good. Creativity is often a matter of rearranging familiar thoughts to discover whole new worlds of meaning and devotion.

Prayer is an adventure. It does change you. It does enlarge your mind and throw new shafts of light onto set ideas and conventional assumptions. Do expect God to change you, and then he will!

RICHARD GARRARD

Special thanks are due to Mrs Jean Wickham for typing of drafts, comments and unfailing good humour.

a time to Pray

GOD IN ALL CREATION

A reflection based on the words of William Blake

FROM VALA OR THE FOUR ZOAS

> For whether they looked upward:
> **They saw the Divine Vision:**
> Or whether they looked downward:
> **Still they saw the Divine Vision:**
> Surrounding them on all sides:
> **Beyond sin and death and hell.**

READING JOB 42:1-6. T.E.V.

> Job answered the Lord:

I know, Lord, that you are all powerful;
  that you can do everything you want.
You ask how I dare question your wisdom
  when I am very ignorant.
I talked about things I did not understand,
  about marvels too great for me to know.
You told me to listen while I spoke
  and to try to answer your questions.
In the past I knew only what others had told me,
  but now I have seen you with my own eyes.
So I am ashamed of all I have said
  and repent in dust and ashes.

READING BLAKE ATTACKS THE ATHEISM OF HIS DAY

> Mock on, Mock on Voltaire, Rousseau:
> Mock on, Mock on: 'tis all in vain!
> You throw the sand against the wind,
> And the wind blows it back again.
>
> And every sand becomes a Gem
> Reflected in the beams divine;
> Blown back they blind the mocking Eye,
> But still in Israel's paths they shine.

The Atoms of Democritus
And Newton's Particles of light
Are sands upon the Red Sea shore,
Where Israel's tents do shine so bright.

PICTURE • PONDER • PRAY • PROMISE

Lord God Creator, nature expresses your grandeur:
We adore you.
Lord God, majestic in space, glorious in proton
and neutron:
We adore you.
Lord God, mighty in power, gentle in motherhood:
We adore you.
Lord God, perfect in love, endless in being:
We adore you.
Lord God, you have given mankind a wonderful
home:
Grant us grace to use your gifts with wisdom.
Lord God, you have given us yourself in Jesus:
May your spirit guide us in all we are and we do.

Blake wrote *Vala* between 1797 and 1804. *Mock on* was published circa 1803.

GOD IS TRUTH

A reflection on the demanding search for truth

JOHN 8:31. T.E.V.

> Jesus said to those who believed in him:
> 'If you obey my teaching, you are really my
>   disciples;
> You will know the truth,
> And the truth will set you free.'

READING BERTRAND RUSSELL, ATHEIST PHILOSOPHER,
CALLS FOR RIGOROUS TRUTHFULNESS IN ALL
THINKING.

When you are studying any matter or considering any philosophy, ask yourself only what are the facts and what is the truth that the facts bear out. Never let yourself be diverted either by what you would wish to believe or by what you think would have beneficial social effects if it were believed. But look only at what are the facts.

READING PSALM 26

Give judgement for me O Lord
for I have walked in my integrity:
>   I have trusted in the Lord and not wavered.

Put me to the test O Lord and prove me:
>   try my mind and my heart.

For your steadfast love has been ever before my eyes:
>   and I have walked in your truth.

I have not sat with deceivers:
>   nor consorted with the hypocrites;

I hate the assembly of the wicked:
>   I will not sit with the ungodly.

I wash my hands in innocence O Lord:
>   that I may go about your altar,

and lift up the voice of thanksgiving:
  to tell of all your marvellous works.

Lord I love the house of your habitation:
  and the place where your glory dwells.

Do not sweep me away with sinners:
  nor my life with men of blood,

in whose hand is abomination:
  and their right hand is full of bribes.

As for me, I walk in my integrity:
  O ransom me and be favourable toward me.

My foot stands on an even path:
  I will bless the Lord in the great congregation.

PICTURE • PONDER • PRAY • PROMISE

Lord, help us to seek the truth in all life:
make us strong to obey the truth.
Lord, give us courage to speak truth to others:
and to love to honour your truth.
Lord, may we always defend what is true:
and follow the truth to the end. Amen.

The source of the quotation from Bertrand Russell is unknown.

GOD IS . . .

What is God like? We reflect on this, and upon humanity's search for the answer

FROM PSALM 42:1-4

As a deer longs for the running brooks:
so longs my soul for you, O God.
My soul is thirsty for the living God:
when shall I come and see his face?

READING A POEM ON GOD'S INFINITE GREATNESS AND HIS
LOVE FOR EACH PERSON

God is a blob
an amoeba-like blob
elongating
fissioning
stretching
extending in limitless space.
Far from the confines
of the earth and its peoples,
aeons away from the man on the street –
from the thousands of men on the street –
billions of light years
removed from us all,
how could he fashion the soul so small?
In his infinite process of changing and growing,
what does he know of our little knowing?
How could he care for the tears of our caring?
or answer with love the love we are daring?
Exploding atoms in galaxy form
star distance away
move the god who is gone.
Yet mysteries baffle the mind left behind
and I who am so strongly I
feel warmly encroached upon.

READING: ACTS 17:22-31. T.E.V. ST. PAUL DECLARES JESUS
TO BE THE VITAL CLUE THAT LEADS TO GOD

Paul stood up in front of the city council and said, 'I see that in every way you Athenians are very religious. For as I walked through your city and looked at the places where you worship, I found an altar on which is written, "To an Unknown God". That which you worship, then, even though you do not know it, is what I now proclaim to you.

God, who made the world and everything in it, is Lord of heaven and earth and does not live in man-made temples. Nor does he need anything that we can supply by working for him, since it is he himself who gives life and breath and everything else to everyone. From one man he created all races of mankind and made them live throughout the whole earth. He himself fixed beforehand the exact times and the limits of the places where they would live. He did this so that they would look for him, and perhaps find him as they felt about for him.

Yet God is actually not far away from any one of us; as someone has said:

"In him we live and move and exist"

It is as some of your poets have said:

"We too are his children."

Since we are God's children, we should not suppose that his nature is anything like an image of gold or silver or stone, shaped by the art and skill of man. God has overlooked the times when people did not know him, but now he commands all of them everywhere to turn away from their evil ways. For he has fixed a day in which he will judge the whole world with justice by means of a man he has chosen. He has given proof of this to everyone by raising that man from death!'

PICTURE • PONDER • PRAY • PROMISE

Infinite God, too great for words:
We adore your infinite greatness.
Infinite God, in all that exists:
We adore your closeness to you.
Infinite God, perfect in love:
We respond to your love with our hearts.
The Lord is King:
Let all creation be glad for ever!

The First reading is from *Protest in Semantics*, by Betty Atkins Fukuyama, published in *The United Church Herald* in 1967. Copyright control.

GOD IS LOVE

God's love and our calling to share love

How good to give thanks to the Lord:
To sing praises to your name O Most High.
To declare your love in the morning:
And at night to sing of your faithfulness.

READING 1 CORINTHIANS 13. T.E.V. ST PAUL TALKS OF
LOVE, THE KEY TO TRUE LIVING

I may be able to speak the languages of men and even of angels, but if I have no love, my speech is no more than a noisy gong or a clanging bell. I may have the gift of inspired preaching; I may have all knowledge and understand secrets; I may have all the faith needed to move mountains – but if I have no love, I am nothing. I may give away everything I have, and even give up my body to be burnt – but if I have no love, this does me no good.

Love is patient and kind; it is not jealous or conceited or proud; love is not ill-mannered or selfish or irritable; love does not keep a record of wrongs; love is not happy with evil, but is happy with the truth. Love never gives up; and its faith, hope, and patience never fail.

Love is eternal. There are inspired messages, but they are temporary; there are gifts of speaking in strange tongues, but they will cease; there is knowledge, but it will pass. For our gifts of knowledge and of inspired messages are only partial; but when what is perfect comes, then what is partial will disappear.

When I was a child, my speech, feelings, and thinking were all those of a child; now that I am a man, I have no more use for childish ways. What we see now is like a dim image in a mirror; then we shall see face to face. What I know now is only partial; then it will be complete – as complete as God's knowledge of me.

Meanwhile these three remain: faith, hope and love; and the greatest of these is love.

READING HOW CAN WE LOVE AS GOD LOVES?

The Disciple

Grant me, Lord, to spread true light in the world.

Grant that by me and by your children it may
penetrate a little into all
circles, all societies, all economic and political
systems, all laws,
all contracts, all rulings;

Grant that it may penetrate into offices, factories,
apartment buildings,
cinemas, dance halls;

Grant that it may penetrate the hearts of men and that I
may never forget
that the battle for a better world is a battle of love in
the service of love.

Help me to love, Lord, not to waste my powers of love,

To love myself less and less in order to love more and
more,

That around me, no one should suffer or die because I
have stolen the love they needed to live.

God replies

Son, you will never succeed in putting enough love
into the heart
of man and into the world,

For man and the world are hungry for an infinite love.

And God alone can love with boundless love.

But if you want, son, I give you my life,

Draw it within you.

I give you my heart, I give it to my sons.

Love with my heart, son,

And all together you will feed the world, and you will
save it.

PICTURE • PONDER • PRAY • PROMISE

A PRAYER

> Help us to love with your heart, O Lord,
> to feed the world and save it,
> through Jesus Christ our Lord. Amen.

Pray for those whom you love
> for those whom you find it hard to love,
> for those who have no one to love them.

> Let us love one another:
> **For love is of God.**
> Who does not love does not know God:
> **For God is love.**

The opening response is from Psalm 92:1-2
The second reading is from *Prayers of Life*, by Michel Quoist, 1963,
Gill and Macmillan Publishers, Dublin. Reproduced by permission.

GOD: INEXHAUSTIBLY GREAT

God is most surely known when we adore
his infinite greatness

O Lord, open our lips:
To adore your infinite greatness.
You are greater than our greatest thoughts:
Nearer than our smallest wish.

READING   ADORATION AND RELIGION

You want to be truthful to find the truth, to be truthful to find God. We can't eliminate all difficulties. Some people don't want the truth. They get into the train to travel there, but they won't go all the way: they get out in a potato field. These people make scepticism; they sophisticate the mind. We are like sponges trying to mop up the ocean. We can never know God exhaustively. God is simultaneous . . . We are passing . . . We can never picture God or imagine him. Either we make him too small and we strain at that, or we make him too big, and he strains us. Let us rest content. We have not got to invent God, not to hold him. He holds us. We shall never be able to explain God, though we can apprehend him more and more through the spiritual life. I want you to hold very clearly the otherness of God, and the littleness of men. If you don't get that you can't have adoration, and you can't have religion without adoration.

READING   ISAIAH 40:8-26. R.E.B.

What likeness, then, will you find for God
   or what form to resemble his?
An image which a craftsman makes,
      and a goldsmith overlays with gold and fits with studs
         of silver?
Or should someone choose mulberry-wood,
      a wood that does not rot,

and seek out a skilful craftsman for the task
of setting up an image and making it secure?

Do you not know, have you not heard,
were you not told long ago?
Have you not perceived ever since the world was
founded,
that God sits enthroned on the vaulted roof of the
world,
and its inhabitants appear as grasshoppers?
He stretches out the skies like a curtain,
spreads them out like a tent to live in;
he reduces the great to naught
and makes earthly rulers as nothing.
Scarcely are they planted, scarcely sown,
scarcely have they taken root in the ground,
before he blows on them and they wither,
and a whirlwind carries them off like chaff.

To whom, then, will you liken me,
whom set up as my equal?
asks the Holy One.
Lift up your eyes to the heavens;
consider who created these,
led out their host one by one,
and summoned each by name.
Through his great might, his strength and power,
not one is missing.

PICTURE · PONDER · PRAY · PROMISE

Pray to grow more deeply reverent of the God
who is infinitely great.

Pray for those who are gripped by their own importance
and for those who feel too small to matter.

Pray for a sense of God's greatness and his concern
for all people.

Blessed be the name of the Lord:
Now and evermore.
From the rising of the sun to its setting:
May the Lord's name be praised.
High is the Lord above all nations:
His glory above the heavens.
No one has ever seen God:
But God's only Son.
He who is nearest to the Father's heart:
Has made him known.

The first reading is from *Letters to a Niece* by F. von Hügel, published by Dent, 1928. Reproduced by permission.
The concluding response is adapted from Psalm 113:2-4 and John 1:18. R.E.B.

FOCUS ON GOD

*A reflection on two ways of seeing
the physical and the spiritual*

O Lord, open our lips:
To adore you, the King of truth.
Christ is the light of the world:
In him is no darkness at all.

READING   MY NEW EYES

A medical examination at school had revealed the fact that
I was short-sighted. The doctor took me solemnly between
his knees, looked into my face, and said, 'If you don't get
some glasses, you'll be blind by the time you are fifteen,
and I shall tell your parents so.'

I was rather proud of this distinction. Fifteen. That was
so far ahead that it meant nothing to me. My parents
thought otherwise, and one Saturday afternoon I was
taken to the Chemist's shop. Behind the shop was a room
where my eyes were tested in the rough and ready way
customary in those days. The chemist hung an open
framework that felt like the Forth Bridge around my ears
and on my nose. Lenses were slotted into this, and twisted
about, while I was instructed to read the card of letters
beginning with a large E.

I remember still the astonishment with which I saw the
smaller letters change from a blur into separate items of
the alphabet. I thought about it all the following week,
and found that by screwing up my eyes when I was out of
doors I could get to some faint approximation of that
clarity, for a few seconds at a time. This made me surmise
that the universe which hitherto I had seen as a vague
mass of colour and blurred shapes might in actuality be
much more concise and defined. I was therefore half
prepared for the surprise which shook me a week later
when, on the Saturday evening, we went again to the
shop, and the chemist produced the pair of steel-rimmed

spectacles through which I was invited to read the card. I read it, from top to bottom! I turned and looked in triumph at Mother, but what I saw was Mother intensified. I saw the pupils of her eyes, the tiny features in her boa necklet; I saw the hair in Father's moustache, and on the back of his hand. Jack's cap might have been made of metal, so hard and clear did it shine on his close-cropped head, above his bony face and huge nose. I saw his eyes too, round, enquiring fierce with a hunger of observation. He was studying me with a gimlet sharpness such as I had never before been able to perceive.

Then we walked out of the shop, and I stepped on to the pavement, which came up and hit me, so that I had to grasp the nearest support – Father's coat.'Take care now, take care!' he said, 'And mind you don't break them!'

I walked still with some uncertainty, carefully placing my feet and feeling their impact on the pavement whose surface I could see sparkling like quartz in the lamplight.

The lamplight! I looked in wonder at the diminishing crystals of gas flame strung down the hill. Clapham was hung with necklaces of light, and the horses pulling the glittering omnibuses struck the granite road with hooves of iron and ebony. I could see the skeletons inside the flesh and blood of the Saturday-night shoppers. The garments they wore were made of separate threads. In this new world, sound as well as sight was changed. It took on hardness and definition, forcing itself upon my hearing, so that I was besieged simultaneously through the eye and through the ear.

READING JOHN 14:7-14. R.E.B.
JESUS, THE DIVINE LENS OF GOD

'If you knew me you would know my Father too. From now on you do know him; you have seen him.' Philip said to him, 'Lord, show us the Father; we ask no more.' Jesus answered, 'Have I been all this time with you, Philip, and still you do not know me? Anyone who has seen me has seen the Father. Then how can you say, 'Show us the

Father'? Do you not believe that I am in the Father, and the Father in me? I am not myself the source of the words I speak to you: it is the Father who dwells in me doing his own work. Believe me when I say that I am in the Father and the Father in me; or else accept the evidence of the deeds themselves. In very truth I tell you, whoever has faith in me will do what I am doing; indeed he will do greater things still because I am going to the Father. Anything you ask in my name I will do, so that the Father may be glorified in the Son. If you ask anything in my name I will do it.

PICTURE · PONDER · PRAY · PROMISE

Thank God for Jesus who is our focus on the heart of God
— for all who make God's truth and love real to us.

Pray for evangelists, for all Christians, that we may make
the truth of God clear for others to see,
for theologians, for preachers,
for teachers of every kind.

> No-one has ever seen God:
> **Yet Christ has made him known.**
> We live in the light of Christ:
> **Thanks be to God.**

The first reading is from *Over the Bridge* by Richard Church, Laurence Pollinger Ltd. Reproduced by permission of the Estate of Richard Church.

GOD IS IN ALL THAT HE CREATES

*A reflection on how we can see God
in what he makes in his world*

In the beginning:
God created the heavens and the earth.
The earth was without form and void:
Darkness on the face of the deep.
Yet the Spirit of God was moving:
Over the face of the waters.

READING GENESIS 1:24-31. T.E.V.

God commanded, 'Let the earth produce all kinds of animal life: domestic and wild, large and small' – and it was done. So God made them all, and he was pleased with what he saw.

Then God said, 'And now we will make human beings; they will be like us and resemble us. They will have power over the fish, the birds, and all animals, domestic and wild, large and small.' So God created human beings, making them to be like himself. He created them male and female, blessed them, and said, 'Have many children, so that your descendants will live all over the earth and bring it under their control. I am putting you in charge of the fish, the birds, and all the wild animals. I have provided all kinds of grain and all kinds of fruit for you to eat; but for all the wild animals and for all the birds I have provided grass and leafy plants for food' – and it was done. God looked at everything he had made, and he was very pleased. Evening passed and morning came – that was the sixth day.

READING WINTER WALK AT NOON

There lives and works
A soul in all things, and that soul is God.
The beauties of the wilderness are his,
That make so gay the solitary place

Where no eye sees them. And fairer forms
That cultivation glories in, are his.
He sets the bright procession on its way,
And marshals all the order of the year;
He marks the bounds which winter may not pass,
And blunts its pointed fury; in its case,
Russet and rude, folds up the tender germ,
Uninjured, with inimitable art;
And, ere one flowery season fades and dies,
Designs the blooming wonders of the next.

The Lord of all, himself through all diffused,
Sustains, and is the life of all that lives.
Nature is but a theme for an effect
Whose cause is God.

PICTURE • PONDER • PRAY • PROMISE

A PRAYER

Lord God, you have given mankind
a most wonderful home;
give us also the wisdom to use it to your glory
as stewards of your precious gifts. Amen.

Praise God for his creation, especially for those parts
of it which you enjoy most.

Pray for the governments of the world in their care
of the life of the earth.

Pray for each human being that they may have enough
of the good things in life to make them
be thankful to God.

Eternal Father, revealed in Creation:
We worship and adore you.
Lord, make us faithful stewards of life and love:
Through Christ our only Saviour, Friend and King.

The first reading is an extract from a longer poem of the same name by William
Cowper. The opening verse is based on Genesis 1:1 & 2 R.S.V.

GOD IN ALL LIFE

God is immediate to those who are willing
to see him in what, and in whom, we know

There is a book, who runs may read:
Which heavenly truth imparts.
And all the lore its scholars need:
Pure eyes and Christian hearts.
The works of God, above, below:
Within us and around,
Are pages in that book to show:
How God himself is found.

READING 1 JOHN 1:1-7. T.E.V.

We write to you about the Word of Life, which has existed
from the very beginning. We have heard it, and we have
seen it with our eyes: yes, we have seen it, and our hands
have touched it. When this life became visible, we saw it;
so we speak of it and tell you about the eternal life which
was with the Father and was made known to us. What we
have seen and heard we announce to you also, so that you
will join with us in the fellowship that we have with the
Father and with his Son Jesus Christ. We write this in order
that our joy may be complete.

Now the message that we have heard from his Son and
announce is this: God is light, and there is no darkness at
all in him. If, then, we say that we have fellowship with
him, yet at the same time live in darkness, we are lying
both in our words and in our actions. But if we live in the
light – just as he is in the light – then we have fellowship
with one another, and the blood of Jesus, his Son, purifies
us from every sin.

READING DIETRICH BONHOEFFER SPEAKS ON GOD'S
PRESENCE IN DAILY LIFE

It has again been brought home to me quite clearly how wrong it is to use God as a stop-gap for the incompleteness of our knowledge. If in fact the frontiers of knowledge are being pushed further and further back (and this is bound to be the case), then God is being pushed back with them, and is, therefore, continually in retreat. We are to find God in what we know, not what we do not know; God wants us to realize his Presence, not in unsolved problems, but in those that are solved.

PICTURE • PONDER • PRAY • PROMISE

A PRAYER

Lord, give us eyes to see you everywhere,
through Jesus Christ our Lord. Amen.

We shall find God:
In what we know.
We shall find God:
In whom we meet.
Let us go in peace:
To love and serve the Lord.

The second reading is from *Letters & Papers from Prison*, the Enlarged Edition, Dietrich Bonhoeffer, 1971, SCM Press. Reproduced by permission.

God's Grandeur

*God's glory seen in creation and nature's
resilience against mankind's lack of care for God's will*

O Lord, open our lips:
To praise you, Creator and Father.
Creation declares your glory:
We bless you for all you have made.

READING COLOSSIANS 1:15-20. J.B.
CHRIST IS THE HEAD OF ALL CREATION

He is the image of the unseen God
    and the first-born of all creation,
    for in him were created
    all things in heaven and on earth:
Everything visible and everything invisible,
    Thrones, Dominations, Sovereignties, Powers –
    all things were created through him and for him.
Before anything was created, he existed,
    and he holds all things in unity.
Now the Church is his body,
    he is its head.

As he is the Beginning,
    he was first to be born from the dead,
    so that he should be first in every way;
    because God wanted all perfection
    to be found in him
And all things to be reconciled through him and for him,
    everything in heaven and everything on earth,
    when he made peace
    by his death on the cross.

READING 'GOD'S GRANDEUR'

The world is charged with the grandeur of God;
    It will flame out, like a shining from shook foil;
    It gathers to a greatness, like the ooze of oil
Crushed, why do men then not reck his rod?
Generations have trod, have trod, have trod;
    And all is seared with trade; bleared, smeared
        with toil;
    And wears man's smudge and shares man's smell:
        the soil
is bare now, nor can foot feel, being shod.

And for all this, nature is never spent;
    There lives the dearest freshness deep down things;
And though the last lights of the black west went
    Oh, morning, at the brown brink eastward springs –
Because the Holy Ghost over the bent
    World broods with warm breast and with ah!
        Bright wings.

PICTURE • PONDER • PRAY • PROMISE

Father, Lord and God, let the endless glory
    of your life:
Find reflection in our lives.
As sun and moon give beauty to land and sea:
May we reflect your glory.
As your Spirit draws us into fellowship:
May your Church reflect your glory.
For your Kingdom is all of creation:
For ever and ever. Amen.

The second reading is by Gerard Manley Hopkins (1844-1889)

GOD'S COSMOS AND HUMAN RESPONSIBILITY

*A reflection on human power
for good and evil*

WORDS BY WILLIAM BLAKE

To see a World in a grain of sand,
And a Heaven in a wild flower,
Hold infinity in the palm of your hand,
And Eternity in an hour.

Almighty Creator, maker of all things:
We adore your endless beauty.
Almighty Creator, maker of all things:
You have created mankind.
Almighty Creator, maker of all things:
Teach us to reverence your universe.

READING WINDSCALE (WRITTEN AFTER
AN ACCIDENT IN A NUCLEAR
POWER STATION)

The toadstool towers infest the shore:
Stink-horns that propagate and spore
    wherever the wind blows.
Scafell looks down from the bracken band,
And sees hell in a grain of sand,
    and feels the canker itch between his toes.

This is the land where dirt is clean,
And poison pasture, quick and green,
And storm sky, bright and bare;
Where sewers flow with milk, and meat
Is carved up for the fire to eat,
And children suffocate in God's fresh air.

READING GALATIANS 6:7-10. R.E.B. A SPIRITUAL
TEACHING BASED ON THE LAWS OF NATURE.

Make no mistake about this: God is not to be fooled;
everyone reaps what he sows. If he sows in the field of his
unspiritual nature, he will reap from it a harvest of
corruption; but if he sows in the field of the Spirit, he will
reap from it a harvest of eternal life. Let us never tire of
doing good, for if we do not slacken our efforts we shall in
due time reap our harvest. Therefore, as opportunity
offers, let us work for the good of all, especially members
of the household of the faith.

PICTURE • PONDER • PRAY • PROMISE

Praise God for the power he has given to human beings:
Pray for its wise use.

Praise God for the benefits of science and technology:
Pray for deep reverence and care in their use.

Praise God for the progress of medical sciences:
Pray for respect for all human lives.

Praise God for mankind's advances in agriculture:
Pray for a fair distribution of food among all people.

Praise God for the science and technology
   in home and at work:
Pray to use it for him, as his steward.

God our maker:
Give us eyes to see you.
Majestic in storms and in mountains:
We reverence your energy.
Glorious in atoms and molecules:
We adore your subtlety.
God our maker:
We are your stewards. Amen.

The first reading is from *A Local Habitation*, by Norman Nicholson, published by
Faber and Faber. Reproduced by permission of David Higham Associates.

THE MYSTERY OF TIME

*A reflection on the mystery of time,
its rhythms and its transience*

O Lord, open our lips:
To praise you, the Lord of Time.
O Lord, open our minds:
To adore you, the God eternal.

READING ECCLESIASTES 3:1-8 R.E.B.
THE SEASONS OF HUMAN LIVING

For everything its season, and for every activity
under heaven its time:

a time to be born and a time to die;
a time to plant and a time to uproot;
a time to kill and a time to heal;
a time to break down and a time to build up;
a time to weep and a time to laugh;
a time for mourning and a time for dancing;
a time to scatter stones and a time to gather them;
a time to embrace and a time to abstain from
embracing;
a time to seek and a time to lose;
a time to keep and a time to discard;
a time to tear and a time to mend;
a time for silence and a time for speech;
a time to love and a time to hate;
a time for war and a time for peace.

READING ALL TIME BELONGS TO GOD

Time that is measured with our clocks does not give a
correct conception of actual time, for it is not a constant
hollow space into which one can stuff the events of life,
one after the other, like books on a bookshelf. It is more
accurately the personal structure of each existing life. On
this basis we make bold to say that time like life itself is

not our private property, but belongs to God and is loaned
to us by him.

PICTURE · PONDER · PRAY · PROMISE

Praise God whose thoughts and ways are greater than
   human brains can comprehend.

Pray for good stewardship of time.

> Lord, giver of time:
> **Help us to travel your world in faith and trust.**
> Lord, creator of time:
> **Let us live with humility.**
> Lord, as you were lifeless on the cross:
> **May we live in you, risen in glory. Amen.**

The second reading is from *Have Time and be Free*, by Theodore Bovet, 1963.
SPCK. Reproduced by permission.

GOD'S FRUITFUL EARTH

Human multiplication and human responsibility

O Lord, open our lips:
To praise you, our Father Creator.
All that exists is yours:
From the beginning and for ever.
The heavens declare your glory:
The earth is the work of your hands.
May we know you in truth today:
And live in your love for ever.

READING GENESIS 1:26-31. J.B.
GOD GIVES MANKIND MASTERY OVER THE EARTH

God said, 'Let us make man in our own image, in the likeness of ourselves, and let them be masters of the fish of the sea, the birds of heaven, the cattle, all the wild beasts and all the reptiles that crawl upon the earth.'

> God created man in the image of himself,
> in the image of God he created him,
> male and female he created them.

God blessed them, saying to them, 'Be fruitful, multiply, fill the earth and conquer it. Be masters of the fish of the sea, the birds of heaven and all living animals on the earth.' God said, 'See, I give you all the seed-bearing plants that are upon the whole earth, and all the trees with seed-bearing fruit; this shall be your food . To all wild beasts, all birds of heaven and all living reptiles on the earth I give all the foliage of plants for food.' And so it was. God saw all he had made, and indeed it was very good.

READING MANKIND AND PLANET EARTH

Planet earth is 4,600 million years old. If we condense this inconceivable time-span into an understandable concept, we can liken Earth to a person of 46 years of age.

Nothing is known about the first 7 years of this person's life, and whilst only scattered information exists about the middle span, we know that only at the age of 42 did the Earth begin to flower.

Dinosaurs and the great reptiles did not appear until one year ago, when the planet was 45. Mammals arrived only 8 months ago; in the middle of last week man-like apes evolved into ape-like men, and at the weekend the last ice-age enveloped the Earth.

Modern man has been around for 4 hours. During the last hour, man discovered agriculture. The industrial revolution began a minute ago.

During those 60 seconds of biological time, modern man has made a rubbish tip of Paradise.

He has multiplied his numbers to plague proportions, caused the extinction of 500 species of animal, ransacked the planet for fuels and now stands like a brutish infant, gloating over his meteoric rise to ascendancy, on the brink of a war to end all wars and of effectively destroying this oasis of life in the solar system.

PICTURE · PONDER · PRAY · PROMISE

Praise and thank God who has entrusted his Earth
    to mankind.

Consider with repentance our own misuse of
    God's creativity.

Pray for those who research the past, present
    and future of the Earth.

Pray for a sense of human stewardship on God's Earth
    and for peace, humility and understanding
    between people.

A Prayer

This planet is not ours, O Lord, it belongs to you.
Our very lives are not ours, we need your
 sustaining power for life, breath, food, everything.
Teach us, O Lord, to live with reverence on the face of
 the Earth which you have made. Amen.

The heavens declare the glory of God:
And the firmament proclaims his handiwork.
The law of the Lord is perfect, reviving the soul:
**The command of the Lord is true and makes wise
 the simple.**
Keep your servants, Lord, from presumptuous sins:
Lest they get the mastery over us.
May the words of our mouths and the meditation
 of our hearts:
Be acceptable in your sight.
You are our strength:
And you are our redeemer.

The second reading is from a Greenpeace pamphlet, 1989. Copyright Greenpeace Ltd, reproduced by permission.

The final response is from Psalm 19 verses 19:1,7, 13 & 14. Slightly adapted.

THE HUMANITY OF GOD

A reflection on the perfect humanity of Jesus

PSALM 8:1,4,5 & 10

O Lord our Governor:
how glorious is your name in all the earth!
When I consider your heavens, the work of your
fingers:
**the moon and the stars which you have set in
order,**
What is man that you should be mindful of him:
or the son of man that you should care for him?
O Lord our Governor:
how glorious is your name in all the earth!

READING HEBREWS 4:14-16. R.E.B.

Since we have a great high priest who has passed through
the heavens, Jesus the Son of God, let us hold fast to the
faith we profess. Ours is not a high priest unable to
sympathise with our weaknesses, but one who has been
tested in every way as we are, only without sinning. Let
us therefore boldly approach the throne of grace, in order
that we may receive mercy and find grace to give us
timely help.

READING THE HUMANITY OF JESUS

The humanity of Jesus was and is a humanity which
dares to be itself in complete openness to other people: He
had the 'courage to be'. Never in the course of the Gospel
story was he putting on an act. He had no self for one
situation and another self for another.

He did not see people as 'contacts';
He did not try to possess or smother other people
with his emotions;
He did not lump people into a group;
He did not love them for what they might become.

He was neither solemn, nor superficial;
He cared nothing for class distinctions or accents;
He was not impressed by power and worldly position;
He was capable of irony, laughter and tears.

He could be angry;
He could shrink naturally from pain;
He could be very outspoken;
He never complained.

He was always true to the truth;
He lived by the love he proclaimed;
He was, in one sense, always an outsider to the world;
He was also the worldly man par excellence.

He was born outside normal convention,
    'no room at the inn',
He died outside normal convention on a cross;
He did not stick close to his family;
He did not abuse his position in society,

He was careless about his reputation when an ex-tart
    joined his followers
He did not worry that people might think him
homosexual by going round with a group of men;
He was an outsider, but at home with all people.
He accepted the hospitality of Simon the Pharisee,
    and of Zaccheus the Publican.

He could speak with equal love on the cross to all;
He spoke to soldiers, criminals, those who jeered him, to
    his mother and his best friend,

As he died in great pain;

This is the Christ relationship;
What Christ was then, he is now in us.

PICTURE • PONDER • PRAY • PROMISE

Jesus perfectly human:
Live through us and in us each day. Amen.
Lord, open our eyes:
To see your world as you see it.
Lord, open our hearts:
To love your world as you love it.

The second reading is adapted from *Prayer in the Secular City*
by D. A. Rhymes, 1967, Lutterworth Press. Reproduced by permission.

GOD'S CREATION AND THE ANIMAL KINGDOM

Human cruelty and divine love

O Lord our Governor:
How glorious is your name in all the earth!
What is man that you should be mindful of him:
Or the son of man that you should care for him?
Yet you have made him little less than a god :
And have crowned him with glory and honour.
You have made him the master of your handiwork:
**And have put all things in subjection beneath
  his feet.**
All sheep and oxen:
And all the creatures of the field.
The birds of the air and the fish of the sea:
**And everything that moves in the pathways of
  the great waters.**
O Lord our Governor:
How glorious is your name in all the earth!

READING GENESIS 2:19-20. J B

From the soil Yahweh God fashioned all the wild beasts
and all the birds of heaven. These he brought to the man to
see what he would call them; each one was to bear the
name the man would give it. The man gave names to all
the cattle, all the birds of heaven and all the wild beasts.

READING A PRAYER FOR ANIMALS OF THE WORLD

Christ Jesus, you are the beginning and the end. In you all
things were created and in you all things are to be
redeemed.

Christ Jesus, you are Lord of Creation. It was for all that
you gave your life on the cross, a perfect sacrifice.

Take, now, to your open arms our grief for
  your creation:

for your wildlife, struggling against extinction:
for the hunted and the trapped:
for the abandoned and the homeless:
for your food animals, unnaturally imprisoned,
    transported and slaughtered in terror:
for your animals used as laboratory tools.

Christ Jesus, in us you live as Risen Lord and our hearts
plead with you now to carry the pain of your suffering
creatures, even to the least of these.

The darkness of the world binds them as it binds us, O
Lord, and only your love can free us to live in your light.

Christ Jesus, come.
Redeem your world. Amen.

PICTURE • PONDER • PRAY • PROMISE

Praise God that in our Lord Jesus Christ we receive light
    and knowledge to live rightly in his world.
Praise God that we are saved from evil by the sacrifice
    of Christ.
Pray that humans may honour the life of God in other
    animals.
Pray that we may use them as food with reverence for
    the gift of God which they are to us.
Pray for all who work in the meat and its allied trades,
    that familiarity with animals may not blunt their
    sensitivity to their beauty and to their suffering.

A PRAYER – THIS CAN BE A RE-READING OF THE
SECOND READING: A PRAYER FOR ANIMALS OF
THE WORLD.

God created mankind in his image:
God is love.
God lets mankind name and use his animals:
May we do this in the love of God.

The opening responses is Psalm 8: 1,5-10.
The second reading is the Alpha and Omega prayer of the Animal Christian
Concern organisation.

OUR FATHER

*To take the phrases of Our Father one by one –
above all in the first part – is to have an idea
of how Christ prayed*

O Lord, open our lips:
To pray with understanding.
O Lord, open our minds:
To pray with sincerity and love.

READING PHILIPPIANS 4:4-7. J.B.
        PRAYER AND PEACE OF MIND

I want you to be happy, always happy in the Lord; I
repeat, what I want is your happiness. Let your tolerance
be evident to everyone: the Lord is very near. There is no
need to worry; but if there is anything you need, pray for
it, asking God for it with prayer and thanksgiving, and
that peace of God, which is so much greater than we can
understand, will guard your hearts and your thoughts, in
Christ Jesus.

READING THOUGHTS ON THE LORD'S PRAYER

      I can pray *Our*:
      if my faith has room for others and their need.
      I can pray *Father*:
      if I live this relationship in daily life.
      I can pray *who art in heaven*:
      if all my interests recall that he is Lord.
      I can pray *hallowed be thy name*:
      if I am striving to be holy.
      I can pray *thy kingdom come*:
      if I am willing to accept God's kingship now.
      I can pray *thy will be done*:
      if I do not resent my need for guidance.
      I can pray *on earth as it is in heaven*:
      if I truly want to serve him here and now.

I can pray *give us this day our daily bread*:
if I work honestly and care for my neighbour's need.
I can pray *forgive us our trespasses as we forgive*
  them that trespass against us:
if I will cancel my grudges and grouses.
I can pray *lead us not into temptation*:
if I remove myself from my own temptations.
I can pray *deliver us from evil*:
if I am willing to fight evil in myself and in life
  about me.
I can pray *thine is the kingdom*:
if I am glad to obey the King of creation.
I can pray *thine is the power and the glory*:
if I am not seeking my own glory and power.
I can pray *for ever and ever*:
if I avoid the anxieties which destroy faith
  and trust.
I can pray *Amen*:
if I want this to be my own true prayer.

PICTURE • PONDER • PRAY • PROMISE

Pray the Lord's Prayer with awareness that faith
  is costly.

Pray it again for people in God's world.

God be within us in heart, deed and voice:
To live for him now, is to live for eternity.

The introductory wording of this order for worship is from *Christian Vocation* by René Voillaume, published Gill, 1973.

The thoughts on the 'Our Father' are adapted from a scheme published anonymously in 1989.

GOD OUR MOTHER

*Awareness is never an end in itself. It only exists
so that more of God, more of love, is created*

God, Father of creation:
We praise and adore you.
Christ, Saviour of creation:
We praise and adore you.
Spirit of nurture and motherhood:
We praise and adore you.

READING THE PARENTHOOD OF GOD

As truly as God is our Father, so just as truly is he our
Mother. In our Father, God Almighty, we have our being;
in our merciful Mother we are remade and restored. Our
fragmented lives are knit together and perfected. And by
giving and yielding ourselves, through grace, to the Holy
Spirit, we are made whole.

READING ROMANS 8:22-27. T.E.V.

We know that up to the present time all of creation groans
with pain, like the pain of childbirth. But it is not just
creation alone which groans; we who have the Spirit as
the first of God's gifts also groan within ourselves, as we
wait for God to make us his sons and set our whole being
free. For it was by hope that we were saved; but if we see
what we hope for, then it is not really hope. For who
hopes for something he sees? But if we hope for what we
do not see, we wait for it with patience.

In the same way the Spirit also comes to help us, weak
as we are. For we do not know how we ought to pray; the
Spirit itself pleads with God for us in groans that words
cannot express. And God, who sees into our hearts,
knows what the thought of the Spirit is; because the Spirit
pleads with God on behalf of his people and in
accordance with his will.

PICTURE • PONDER • PRAY • PROMISE

Praise God that his parenthood is a balanced
and sensitive nurturing of all his people.

Pray to be sensitive to God in all living.

Pray for those whose ideas of God are tyrannical
and oppressive.

A PRAYER

Creator, Saviour, Spirit,
Three persons, one in life and love;
You are more truly real than human brains can know,
More truly great than we can measure with
our minds,
More truly loving than our warmest loving hearts,
Help us to rejoice in you! Amen.

You are our God:
We praise you.
You are alive within us:
We welcome you.
You are our dearest love:
And our eternal home.

The introductory wording of this worship is from *Hearing Ourselves* by Verena Tschudin, published Marshall Pickering, 1989.

The first reading, by Julian of Norwich, is from *Revelations of Divine Love* sections 58 & 59.

In the second reading (Romans 8:26) 'itself' is used in place of 'Himself' in T.E.V. in accordance with the Greek text.

THE HOLY CROSS

*A reflection on Jesus's victory over
evil, sin and death*

O Lord, open our lips:
To praise Christ, crucified for us.
All things are subject to him:
Through him we are one with God.

READING 1 CORINTHIANS 15:20-28. T.E.V.

But the truth is that Christ has been raised from death, as
the guarantee that those who sleep in death will also be
raised. For just as death came by means of man, in the
same way the rising from death comes by means of a
man. For just as all people die because of their union with
Adam, in the same way all will be raised to life because of
their union with Christ. But each one will be raised in his
proper order; Christ, first of all; then, at the time of his
coming, those who belong to him. Then the end will
come; Christ will overcome all spiritual rulers,
authorities, and powers, and will hand over the Kingdom
to God the Father. For Christ must rule until God defeats
all enemies and puts them under his feet. The last enemy
to be defeated will be death. For the scripture says, 'God
put *all* things under his feet.' It is clear, of course, that the
words 'all things' do not include God himself, who puts
all things under Christ. But when all things have been
placed under Christ's rule, then he himself, the Son, will
place himself under God, who placed all things under
him; and God will rule completely over all.

READING THE HOLY CROSS

Christ when he died
Deceived the cross;
And on death's side
Threw all the loss.

The captive world awaked and found
The prisoner loose, the jailer bound.

PICTURE • PONDER • PRAY • PROMISE

Praise God for Jesus, for his conquest of death and evil.

Pray God for people who fear death,
    who cannot believe God loves them,
    who live boring and joyless lives.

> He was crucified:
> **He is risen.**
> He was dead:
> **He is alive for ever.**
> He lives in us today:
> **In his name we live.**

The second reading is by Richard Crawshaw (1612-49)

THE WORD BECAME A HUMAN BEING

How God himself became one of us

O Lord, open our lips:
For we love to sing your praise.
We praise you for your birth:
Born as a human child.

READING JOHN 1:1-14. T.E.V.
THE WORD OF LIFE

Before the world was created, the Word already existed; he was with God, and he was the same as God. From the very beginning the Word was with God. Through him God made all things; not one thing in all creation was made without him. The Word was the source of life, and this life brought light to mankind. The light shines in the darkness, and the darkness has never put it out.

God sent his messenger, a man named John, who came to tell people about the light, so that all should hear the message and believe. He himself was not the light; he came to tell about the light. This was the real light – the light that comes into the world and shines on all mankind.

The Word was in the world, and though God made the world through him, yet the world did not recognise him. He came to his own country, but his own people did not receive him. Some, however, did receive him and believed in him; so he gave them the right to become God's children. They did not become God's children by natural means, that is, by being born as the children of a human father; God himself was their Father.

The Word became a human being and, full of grace and truth, lived among us. We saw his glory, the glory which he received as the Father's only Son.

John spoke about him. He cried out, 'This is the one I was talking about when I said, "He comes after me, but he is greater than I am, because he existed before I was born."'

Out of the fullness of his grace he has blessed us all, giving us one blessing after another. God gave the Law through Moses, but grace and truth came through Jesus Christ. No one has ever seen God. The only Son, who is the same as God and is at the Father's side, he has made him known.

READING HE CAME HIMSELF

He did not send technical assistance
to our backward world;
Gabriel and a company of experts
with their know-how.
He did not negotiate
For the export of surplus grace
On a long term loan.
He did not arrange to send us food
Or the cast-off garment of angels.
Instead, He came himself.
He hungered in the wilderness,
He was stripped naked on the Cross,
But hungering with us
He became our bread,
And suffering for us
He became our Joy.

PICTURE • PONDER • PRAY • PROMISE

A PRAYER

Lord Jesus Christ
You were poor
and in distress, a captive and forsaken as we are.
You know all man's troubles;
You abide with us
when all men fail us;
You remember and seek us;
It is your will that we should know you
and turn to you.
Lord, we hear your call and follow;
Help us.

Praise God for Jesus and for his birth among mankind
   for his divine willingness to share human life
   for his infinite love and compassion for a world
      lost in evil.

Pray for the love of God to rule the hearts and minds
   of the world
   for those whose lives are impoverished,
   boring and hard
   for grace to hear God' s call and to follow him.

God gave the Law through Moses:
Grace and truth through Jesus Christ.
No-one has seen God:
But Jesus has made him known.
We may go in peace:
For we live in the love of the Lord.

The second reading is by Edith Loveday Pierce and was first published in *Christian Century*, March 1955.

The prayer is from *Letters & Papers from Prison*, the Enlarged Edition, by Dietrich Bonhoeffer, 1971, SCM Press. Reproduced by permission.

JESUS: REVOLUTIONARY

The Gospel causes a riot

Your glory, O God, is eternal:
In heaven and earth you are king.
You are wiser than human wisdom:
Stronger than earthly strength.

READING ACTS 17:1-9. T.E.V.

Paul and Silas travelled on through Amphipolis and Apollonia and came to Thessalonica, where there was a synagogue. According to his usual habit Paul went to the synagogue. There during three Sabbaths he held discussions with the people, quoting and explaining the Scriptures and proving from them that the Messiah had to suffer and rise from death. 'This Jesus whom I announce to you,' Paul said, 'is the Messiah.' Some of them were convinced and joined Paul and Silas; so did many of the leading women and a large group of Greeks who worshipped God.

But the Jews were jealous and gathered some of the worthless loafers from the streets and formed a mob. They set the whole city in an uproar and attacked the home of a man called Jason, in an attempt to find Paul and Silas and bring them out to the people. But when they did not find them, they dragged Jason and some other believers before the city authorities and shouted, 'These men have caused trouble everywhere! Now they have come to our city, and Jason has kept them in his house. They are all breaking the laws of the Emperor, saying that there is another king, whose name is Jesus.' With these words they threw the crowd and the city authorities into an uproar. The authorities made Jason and the others pay the required amount of money to be released, and then let them go.

READING THE REVOLUTIONARY JESUS

The Revolutionary Jesus: wanted for challenging norms and traditions. A student magazine in the USA published, some years ago, a picture of Jesus, showing him with the flowing hair of traditional piety. Under the picture was the following statement.

Wanted: for conspiring to obstruct conscription by instructing his followers not to kill:
Matthew 5:39 'I say to you do not resist one who is evil. But if anyone strikes you on the right cheek, turn to him the other also.'

Wanted: for practising medicine without proper qualifications.
Matthew 8:16 They brought to him many who were possessed with demons; and he cast out the spirits with a word, and healed all who were sick.'

Wanted: for wine-making without a licence.
John 2. Jesus said, 'Fill the jars with water.' They filled them to the brim. The steward of the feast tasted the water and called to the bridegroom, 'You have kept the good wine until now.'

Wanted: for interrupting business in a temple.
John 2:15 and 16. 'Making a whip of cords, he drove them all, with the sheep and oxen, out of the temple; and he poured out the coins of the money-changers and overturned their tables. And he told those who sold the pigeons, 'Take these things away; you shall not make my Father's house a house of trade.'

This man would be recognisable as a typical hippie; beard, long hair, sandals, young. He might be met in any slum, love-in or anti-war demonstration; less often, he might be found in a church.

Warning! This man is especially dangerous to the young, and to those of all ages who have spiritual insight into life.

PICTURE • PONDER • PRAY • PROMISE

Praise God for his love and its challenge to our coolness
of heart.
for the gospel of Jesus and its power to challenge our
assumptions and glib ideas.

Pray for insight into the truth of the gospel and how it
affects human life.

Pray for those who suffer for following the way of
the gospel.

Lord, turn this world upside down:
Let your truth remake our lives.
Lord, turn this world upside down:
Let your love be our guide.
Lord, turn this world upside down:
**Let our hopes and our dreams become one with
you. Amen.**

The second reading is adapted from *The Bullet*, a student magazine of
Mary Washington College, USA.

JESUS CRUCIFIED TODAY

*A reflection on how our Lord suffers still
in the suffering of all mankind*

O Lord, open our lips:
And our mouth shall proclaim your praise.
O Lord, open our hearts:
To share your compassion for all.

READING MATTHEW 25:31-46. R.E.B.
THE FINAL JUDGEMENT

Jesus said to his disciples:

'When the Son of Man comes in all his glory and all the angels with him, he will sit on his glorious throne, with all the nations gathered before him. He will separate people into two groups, as a shepherd separates the sheep from the goats; he will place the sheep on his right hand and the goats on the left.

Then the King will say to those on his right, "You have my Father's blessing; come, take possession of the kingdom that has been ready for you since the world was made. For when I was hungry, you gave me food; when thirsty, you gave me drink; when I was a stranger, you took me into your home; when naked, you clothed me; when I was ill, you came to my help; when in prison, you visited me."

Then the righteous will reply, "Lord, when was it that we saw you hungry and fed you, or thirsty and gave you drink, a stranger and took you home, or naked and clothed you? When did we see you ill or in prison, and come to visit you?"

And the king will answer, "Truly, I tell you: anything you did for one of my brothers here, however insignificant, you did for me."

Then he will say to those on his left, "A curse is on you; go from my sight to the eternal fire that is ready for the devil and his angels. For when I was hungry you gave me nothing to eat; when thirsty, nothing to drink; when I was a stranger, you did not welcome me; when I was naked, you did not clothe me; when I was ill and in prison, you did not come to my help."

And they in their turn will reply, "Lord, when was it that we saw you hungry or thirsty or a stranger or naked or ill or in prison, and did nothing for you?"

And he will answer, "Truly I tell you: anything you failed to do for one of these, however insignificant, you failed to do for me."

And they will go away to eternal punishment, but the righteous will enter eternal life.'

READING INDIFFERENCE

When Jesus came to Golgotha they hanged him
    on a tree,
They drove great nails through hands and feet
    and made a Calvary;
They crowned him with a crown of thorns, red were
    his wounds and deep,
For those were crude and cruel days and human flesh
    was cheap.

When Jesus came to Britain now they simply passed
    him by,
They never hurt a hair of him, they only let him die;
For men had grown more tender, and they would not
    give him pain,
They only passed on down the street, and left him in
    the rain.

Still Jesus cried, 'Forgive them, for they know not what
    they do!'
And still it rained the wintry rain that drenched him
    through and through
The crowds went home and left the streets without a
    soul to see,
And Jesus crouched against a wall and cried for
    Calvary.

PICTURE • PONDER • PRAY • PROMISE

A PRAYER

> Lord, your demands are total, your love unconditional,
> and your understanding complete.
> Lord, give us grace to live out the demands of your
> love, for we cannot serve you in our own strength.
> Amen.

Pray for grace to see as Christ sees,
> to love as Christ loves,
> to act as he wills.

Pray for the cheated, the neglected, the homeless,
> the abused, the starving, the tortured, the imprisoned,
> for all whom no-one wants or cares about.

Praise God for his justice, by which he judges us, his total
> fairness and his understanding of us,
> through and through.

> The Lord will say to us:
> **What you did for my brethren, you did for me.**
> Let us go in peace:
> **To see Christ in all mankind.**

The second reading is from *The Unutterable Beauty*, by G.A. Studdert-Kennedy,
Hodder & Stoughton Ltd. There is one slight change in the text, 'Britain now'
replaces the original 'Birmingham'; Not only in Birmingham . . .

JESUS PRESENTED IN THE TEMPLE

*Mary and Joseph obey the Law of Moses
and receive a prophecy*

Blessed be the Lord the God of Israel:
For he has come to his people and set them free.
He has raised up for us a mighty saviour:
Born of the house of his servant David.

READING LUKE 2:22-35. J.B.
JESUS IS DEDICATED TO GOD

And when the day came for them to be purified as laid down by the Law of Moses, they took him up to Jerusalem to present him to the Lord – observing what stands written in the Law of the Lord: Every first-born male must be consecrated to the Lord – and also to offer in sacrifice, in accordance with what is said in the Law of the Lord, a pair of turtledoves or two young pigeons. Now in Jerusalem there was a man named Simeon. He was an upright and devout man; he looked forward to Israel's comforting and the Holy Spirit rested on him. It had been revealed to him by the Holy Spirit that he would not see death until he had set eyes on the Christ of the Lord. Prompted by the Spirit he came to the Temple: and when the parents brought in the child Jesus to do for him what the Lord required, he took him into his arms and blessed God; and he said:

'Now, Master, you can let your servant go in peace,
just as you promised;
because my eyes have seen the salvation
which you have prepared for all the nations to see,
a light to enlighten the pagans
and the glory of your people in Israel.'

As the child's father and mother stood there wondering at the things that were being said about him, Simeon blessed them and said to Mary his mother, 'You see this child: he is destined for the fall and for the rising of many in Israel, destined to be a sign that is rejected – and a sword will pierce your own soul too – so that the secret thoughts of many may be laid bare.'

READING ALBERT SCHWEITZER AND SELF-SACRIFICE

In our time there have been few men more brilliant or versatile than Schweitzer. While still in his twenties he was in the front rank of theologians and philosophers, a famous organist and a recognised authority on Bach. He could have asked so much of life. But he decided that he would devote himself to his art and his studies until he was thirty; then he would train as a doctor and go to Africa to pay what he could of the debt which he felt the white man owes to the coloured. And as he stood on the deck of the ship bringing him home for a brief furlough, he looked back to Africa and said, 'I feel myself humbled, and ask myself how I earned the privilege of carrying on such a work.'

'Whosoever will save his life shall lose it,' said Jesus, 'and whosoever will lose his life for my sake and the Gospel's, the same shall find it.' These men have discovered His secret that real life is in self-giving, not in bargaining.

PICTURE • PONDER • PRAY • PROMISE

Praise God for Jesus's total dedication to his life's work.
Thank God for Christians who have followed Jesus's way.
Thank God for homes, home life and parents.
Pray for families and homes in these days.

A PRAYER

Lord, as Jesus your Son was presented in the Temple, may we present and dedicate ourselves to you. Amen.

God, who calls us to his service:
Is faithful to us.
God, who gives grace to the faithful:
Will preserve and sustain us.
God's service is perfect freedom:
May we find freedom through his strength.

The second reading is from *Facing Life and Death* by L. J. Tizard, Allen & Unwin Ltd, an imprint of HarperCollins Publishers Ltd. Reproduced by permission.

JESUS AT THE HEART OF LIVING

Jesus, the supreme giver of life's true values

O Lord, open our lips:
To praise you, giver of light.
Darkness is not darkness for you:
You bring us the truth for our lives.

READING FACTS AND VALUES IN SEXUALITY

Remember that you're the product of your 'biology' and
of the epoch into which you have been born. We all are,
and we cease to be slaves to inner and outer forces only by
controlling their effects. The young man who says that it
is now time to try intercourse, and gives fine reasons for
it, is usually giving false reasons; his biological impulses
are in fact the reason and he seeks a tolerable excuse for
their indulgence. As for what we are born into, our epoch
is so dominated by mechanical gadgets that we
automatically tend to think of all difficulties as arising
from causes that are technical – a matter of technique. Just
as we look for the cause of an engine failure in a choked
carburettor or a shorting plug, so we tend to think that a
technical failure underlies an unhappy marriage.

Thank heaven the good life does not depend upon
technique, upon calculation, and planning. It depends
upon generosity, tenderness, sensitiveness. Given these,
you can take problems of technique in your stride;
without them, the most trivial of these problems will
defeat you.

READING JOHN 3:16-21. T.E.V.
          JESUS, SOURCE OF TRUE LIGHT FOR LIVING

God loved the world so much that he gave his only Son,
so that everyone who believes in him may not die but
have eternal life. For God did not send his Son into the
world to be its judge, but to be its saviour.

64

Whoever believes in the Son is not judged; but whoever does not believe has already been judged, because he has not believed in God's only Son. This is how the judgement works: the light has come into the world, but people love the darkness rather than the light, because their deeds are evil. Anyone who does evil things hates the light and will not come to the light because he does not want his evil deeds to be shown up. But whoever does what is true comes to the light in order that the light may show that what he did was in obedience to God.

PICTURE · PONDER · PRAY · PROMISE

Praise God for the gift of sexuality to human beings.
Pray for the grace to enjoy his gift to the full.
Pray for those couples whose sexual lives are painful.
Pray for those who feel driven to violence against their
    partners.

> Let your people praise you, O Lord:
> **Set us free to enjoy your gifts.**
> Make us fruitful in love and compassion:
> **Your law is made perfect in love.**

The first reading is from *He and She*, by K.C. Barnes, 1958, Darwen Finlayson Ltd. Reproduced by permission of Phillimore & Co Ltd, Chichester.

JESUS: LIBERATOR

*Jesus is the hope of a world enmeshed in
self-importance, fears and hatreds*

Lord, King and Redeemer:
Help us to adore you.
To you all glory be:
Lord of time and space.
To you belong earth and the heavens:
Lord of eternity.
You will redeem your creation:
And all shall be very well.

READING REVELATION 21:22-22: 5: T.E.V.
A VISION OF ETERNAL LIFE

I did not see a temple in the city, because its temple is the
Lord God Almighty and the Lamb. The city has no need
of the sun or the moon to shine on it, because the glory of
God shines on it, and the Lamb is its lamp. The peoples of
the world will walk by its light, and the kings of the earth
will bring their wealth into it. The gates of the city will
stand open all day; they will never be closed, because
there will be no night there. The greatness and wealth of
the nations will be brought into the city. But nothing that
is impure will enter the city; nor anyone who does
shameful things or tells lies. Only those whose names are
written in the Lamb's book of the living will enter the city.

The angel also showed me the river of the water of life,
sparkling like crystal, and coming from the throne of God
and of the Lamb and flowing down the middle of the
city's street. On each side of the river was the tree of life,
which bears fruit twelve times a year, once each month;
and its leaves are for the healing of the nations. Nothing
that is under God's curse will be found in the city.

The throne of God and of the Lamb will be in the city,
and his servants will worship him. They will see his face,
and his name will be written on their foreheads. There

shall be no more night, and they will not need lamps or sunlight, because the Lord God will be their light, and they will rule as kings for ever and ever.

READING A VISION OF JESUS, GOD'S HARLEQUIN,
            MAKING ALL LIFE NEW

Come, holy harlequin,
Shake the world and
Shock the hyprocrite,
    Rock, love, carry it away,
    Turn it upside down.
Let the feast of love begin,
Let the hungry all come in.
    Rock, love, carry it away,
    Turn it upside down.
Let the rich and mighty wait,
Let the poor go through the gate.
    Rock, love, carry it away
    Turn it upside down.

Come, holy harlequin,
Show the world your
Slapstick liberty.
    Rock, love, carry it away
    Turn it upside down.

Show the crooked how to live,
Be forgiven and forgive.
    Rock, love, carry it away
    Turn it upside down.
Shake the scribe and pharisee
Shatter their monopoly,
    Rock, love, carry it away,
    Turn it upside down.

Come, holy harlequin,
Shake your rags and
Shine like a diamond.
    Rock, love, carry it away,
    Turn it upside down.

Caper with your Columbine,
Turn the water into wine,
    Rock, love, carry it away,
    Turn it upside down.
Teach the crippled how to leap,
Throw their crutches on a heap.
    Rock, love carry it away,
    Turn it upside down.

Rock, love carry it away,
Lift the world up by your levity,
    Rock, love, carry it away,
    Turn it upside down.
Let the children laugh and shout,
Let me in and let me out,
    Rock, love, carry it away,
    Turn it upside down.
Let the carnival begin,
Let me out and let me in,
    Rock, love carry it away,
    Turn it upside down.
Rock, love, carry it away,
Lift the world by your levity,
    Rock, love, carry it away,
    Turn it upside down.

PICTURE • PONDER • PRAY • PROMISE

Thank God that he is God, Lord and perfecter of creation
    he shall reign in love for ever
    the failings and sins of the world will be healed
    neither death, nor life,
    nor angels, nor principalities,
    nor things present, nor things to come,
    nor powers, nor height, nor depth,
    nor anything else in all creation,
    will be able to separate us
    from the love of God in Christ Jesus our Lord.

Pray for those in prison:
    prisons with gates and bars,
    prisons where men and women go for their crimes.
    prisons where people are put through the hatred of
        others,
    prisons of anxiety and fear,
    prisons of addiction to drugs,
    prisons of convention and habit,
    prisons of conventional religion,
    prisons built through the fear of change,
    prisons of illness of mind and body,
    prisons of apathy,
    prisons of despair.

A PRAYER:

    Lord, free our lives through the joy of the risen Christ.
    Amen.

        In Christ is life:
        And his life is the light of mankind.
        His light shines on in the darkness:
        The darkness shall never quench it.
        Christ is our hope:
        And the hope of all creation.

The second reading is from *Green Print for Song*, by Sydney Carter, Stainer & Bell Ltd. Reproduced by permission.

The thanksgiving is based partly on Romans 8:38-39

PICTURING JESUS

Two ways of looking at Jesus

Almighty God, Father, Creator:
We praise you in your glory.
Jesus the Christ, Saviour, Redeemer:
We praise you in your glory.
Spirit of life, Comforter, Counsellor:
We praise you in your glory.

READING COLOSSIANS 1:15-20. J. B.
CHRIST IS THE HEAD OF ALL CREATION

He is the image of the unseen God
and the first-born of all creation,
for in him were created all things in heaven and on earth:
everything visible and everything invisible,
Thrones, Dominations, Sovereignties, Powers –
all things were created through him and for him.
Before anything was created, he existed,
and he holds all things in unity.
Now the Church is his body,
he is its head.

As he is the Beginning,
he was the first to be born from the dead,
so that he should be first in every way;
Because God wanted all perfection
to be found in him
and all things to be reconciled through him and for him,
everything in heaven and everything on earth,
when he made peace by his death on the cross.

READING HOW HAVE YOU PICTURED JESUS?
(AN EXTRACT FROM A STUDENT'S ESSAY)

The pre-supposed images I was given as a child were all
very much in the Sunday school idiom and depicted Jesus
in everyday Jewish attire and this rather led me to regard

Him as an historical character, One who died on the cross for the salvation of mankind, was resurrected and disappeared off the face of the earth, presumably into heaven. However, the Word 'Jesus ' now has a wider, if not quite so explicit connotation for me, as He has become someone whom I can relate to in everyday, modern life and I have come to recognise what I believe to be Jesus in the souls of men today.

I see the Jesus who suffered persecution and humiliation from His fellow Jews in the black immigrant who walks our streets today branded by the colour of his skin. I see Jesus in the mind of the hippy who is striving to find the truth in life by reverting to the simple, unsophisticated life by practising basic communism as did Jesus and the early Christians. I see Jesus in the mind of the homosexual who is overwhelmed with love and passion for his fellow-men. I see Jesus as a revolutionary, one such as Che Guevera whose aim is to force from power all those who are corrupt in order to save his people from exploitation such as the Jews were experiencing under the dictatorship of the Romans; and to-day Jesus might be regarded as a highly dangerous propagandist or anarchist. I also see Jesus as a mystical Master, a kind of guru, who supplies His followers with spiritual needs and comforts.

This concept might differ from the 'good shepherd' image and yet it is my personal opinion, one which creates Jesus as a very real person, alive to-day and it is because I believe that He embodies so many different and conflicting personalities that He does emerge as such a remarkable and exciting person for me, personally.

One might argue that I am not committed to any one particular view of Christ and that I have depicted Him as a man of many facets. However, if Jesus is the presentation of mankind, then I think this is quite a feasible opinion. I believe that many people would converge with my view though with differing conclusions, and others might be horrified at some of my suggestions. But I also believe that Jesus is a very personal part of many people's lives and in some way or other each person touches on an element of truth about Jesus.

PICTURE • PONDER • PRAY • PROMISE

Praise God that Jesus meets all the needs of mankind
– that he is all things to all people without being the property of any point of view.

Pray that people everywhere may find in Jesus their Lord, Friend and Saviour.

Pray for those whose pictures of Jesus so distort and conceal his true nature that they cannot have faith.

A PRAYER:

Thanks be to you, Jesus Christ,
For your constant love,
For your sacrifice upon the cross,
For your victory over sin and death,
For your everlasting life. Amen.

Be our vision of life:
O Lord of truth.
Be the love in our hearts:
O Lord of love.
Be our hope of heaven:
O Lord of eternity.

The second reading is from an essay by a first year student in an introductory essay soon after her course began at Keswick Hall College of Further Education

JESUS THE ENABLER

*A reflection on how the Christian life
is too difficult for men and women*

O Lord, open our lips:
Teach us to praise your name.
O Lord, we need you to save us:
For we cannot save ourselves.
We trust in your grace:
For your power is our hope.

READING A HUMANIST'S TRIBUTE TO JESUS.

Suppose your husband, for some purely imaginary crime, has been sent to forced labour in the Arctic, and has died of cruelty and starvation. Suppose your daughter has been raped and then killed by enemy soldiers. Ought you, in these circumstances, to preserve a philosophic calm?

If you follow Christ's teaching, you will say, 'Father, forgive them, for they know not what they do.' I have known Quakers who could have said this sincerely and profoundly, and whom I admired because they could. But before giving admiration one must be very sure that the misfortune is felt as deeply as it should be. One cannot accept the attitude among some Stoics, who said, "What does it matter to me if my family suffer? I can still be virtuous.' The Christian principle, 'Love your enemies' is good but the Stoic principle 'Be indifferent to your friends' is bad. And the Christian principle does not inculcate calm, but an ardent love even towards the worst of men. There is nothing to be said against it except that it is too difficult for most of us to practise sincerely.

READING JOHN 15:1-10. R.E.B.
JESUS: SOURCE OF LIFE AND STRENGTH

I am the true vine, and my father is the gardener. Any branch of mine that is barren he cuts away; and any fruiting branch he prunes clean, to make it more fruitful still. You are already clean because of the word I have spoken to you. Dwell in me, as I in you. No branch can bear fruit by itself, but only if it remains united with the vine; no more can you bear fruit, unless you remain united with me.

I am the vine; you are the branches. Anyone who dwells in me, as I dwell in him, bears much fruit; apart from me you can do nothing. Anyone who does not dwell in me is thrown away like a withered branch. The withered branches are gathered up, thrown on the fire, and burnt.

If you dwell in me, and my words dwell in you, ask whatever you want, and you shall have it. This is how my Father is glorified: you are to bear fruit in plenty and so be my disciples. As the Father has loved me, so I have loved you. Dwell in my love. If you heed my commands, you will dwell in my love, as I have heeded my Father's commands and dwell in his love.

PICTURE • PONDER • PRAY • PROMISE

A PRAYER

> Jesus, human and divine, conquerer of evil
>   and of death,
> Make us able to live in your way,
> Help us to rise above fear and selfishness,
> Let us think, speak and act each day
> In the power of the Holy Spirit. Amen.

Thank God that we are not confined by the sins and habits
    of our past
    – that in the saints of old and in saints alive today,
    we see the proving of the power of Jesus.

Pray to grow in faith and hope and love, for these are
    the fruits of the Spirit.

Pray for those drowning in sorrow, guilt and despair, that
    they will find the love and power of Jesus.

Pray to abide, to dwell, to live in Jesus and to show him in deeds and and words alive in you today.

And thank God that when we fail his mercy will renew us through Jesus.

Lord of victorious life:
Bring strength out of our weakness.
Lord of mercy and forgiveness:
Bring us true gratitude for your love.
Lord, to whom all is possible:
Heal our lack of faith.

The first reading is from *History of Western Philosophy* by Bertrand Russell, 1946, Allen & Unwin Ltd. Reproduced by permission of Thomson Publishing Services Ltd.

THE COHERENCE OF LIFE
IN JESUS THE CHRIST

*A reflection on the sense of wholeness
and purpose that we can find in faith*

O Lord, open our lips:
And open our hearts and minds.
As Christ has been raised from the tomb:
Fix our lives upon him.

READING A CHAOS OF SPIRITS IN A WORLD WITHOUT GOD

The speaker is Carel, a disillusioned and eccentric priest,
who believes that God is dead:

'If there is goodness it must be one. Multiplicity is not
paganism, it is the triumph of evil, or rather of what used
to be called evil and is now nameless . . . The
disappearance of God does not simply leave a void into
which human reason can move. The death of God has set
the angels free. And they are terrible . . . There are
principalities and powers. Angels are the thoughts of
God. Now he has been dissolved into his thoughts which
are beyond our conception in their nature and their
multiplicity and their power. God was at least the name of
something which we thought was good. Now even the
name has gone and the spiritual world is scattered. There
is nothing any more to prevent the magnetism of many
spirits.'

READING COLOSSIANS 2:6-10. T.E.V.
          JESUS, THE HEART OF CREATION

Since you have accepted Jesus Christ as Lord, live in
union with him. Keep your roots deep in him, build your
lives on him, and become stronger in your faith, as you
were taught. And be filled with thanksgiving.

See to it, then, that no one enslaves you by means of
the worthless deceit of human wisdom, which comes from

the teachings handed down by men and from the ruling spirits of the universe, and not from Christ. For the full content of divine nature lives in Christ, in his humanity, and you have been given full life in union with him. He is supreme over every spiritual ruler and authority.

PICTURE · PONDER · PRAY · PROMISE

Thank God for Jesus who has made God known
   – for the order and truth that Jesus brings to our living
   – for all who find in Jesus the peace and the love
     of God.

Pray for those who have no faith
   – those who have lost their faith
   – those obsessed by witchcraft and 'black arts'.

A PRAYER

   Centre of life, Jesus our Lord and our God,
     be at the centre of our lives. Amen.

     There is one God:
     Father of Creation.
     There is one God:
     Jesus our Lord.
     There is one God:
     The Spirit who inspires us.
     There is one God:
     These Three are one.

The first reading is from *The Time of the Angels*, by Iris Murdoch, Chatto & Windus. Reproduced by permission of Random House UK Ltd.

THE TEMPTATIONS OF JESUS (1)

*The first of three reflections on the temptations
of Jesus as told in St Matthew's Gospel*

The temptations of material well-being

> Father Creator:
> **Jesus Redeemer,**
> Spirit of truth:
> **We praise you for ever.**

READING MATTHEW 4:1-4. R.E.B.
THE FIRST TEMPTATION OF CHRIST

Jesus was then led by the Spirit into the wilderness, to be
tempted by the devil.

For forty days and nights he fasted, and at the end of
them he was famished. The tempter approached him and
said, 'If you are the Son of God, tell these stones to
become bread.' Jesus answered, 'Scripture says, "Man is
not to live on bread alone, but on every word that comes
from the mouth of God."'

READING THE FIRST TEMPTATION TODAY

Our civilization is the richest the world has ever known.
We put bread first. We don't ask, for instance, whether
modern advertising will make people covetous and
discontented. The primary thing for us is to create
markets and increase output. And many of us in our
personal life put bread first. Last year, I watched a
marriage breaking up. Both husband and wife were
working full time, and he was doing all the overtime he
could get. They were doing well and getting on. But they
never saw each other except for bed and breakfast. Is it
any wonder that they drifted apart, and that, with the
deeper hunger in her nature for relationship, she began to
find outside her marriage what she wasn't finding in it?

But below the surface is the hunger that bread can never satisfy. Take our crazy wages spiral. Every time you open your newspaper there's a wage claim or a strike in the offing. We know that wage increases mean price increases, which mean that we're no better off in the end. But we still go on holding each other to ransom. Why do we do it? Could it be that at the root of the situation there is a spiritual hunger which the wage increase does nothing to satisfy? Could it be that what different sections of the community are saying to the rest is, 'You don't value us enough, you don't care about us enough to give us justice?'

Jesus saw that bread is vital. He is also saw that the life bread gives only becomes worth living when bread is put second to the love and worship of God.

PICTURE · PONDER · PRAY · PROMISE

Praise God the giver of all material good.

Pray for sensitivity in the using of wealth and possessions and for those who starve whilst we are well-fed.

A PRAYER

> Giver of bread and all good things,
> Deliver us from the evils of materialism,
> For we are stewards, not owners, of your world. Amen.

> Son of God, who learned obedience
>   through suffering:
> **Keep us firm in faith when we are tested.**
> Son of God, made perfect through trial and
>   temptation:
> **Keep us in the truth; your word is truth.**

The second reading is from *To Me Personally* by Wilf Wilkinson, published by Fontana, 1972, HarperCollins Publishers, London. Reproduced by permission.

The Temptations of Jesus (2)

*The second of three reflections on the temptations
of Jesus as told in St Matthew's Gospel*

The temptations to compel belief by signs and wonders.

> Father Creator:
> **Jesus Redeemer,**
> Spirit of truth:
> **We praise you for ever.**

Reading Matthew 4:5-7. R.E.B.
The second temptation of Christ

The devil then took him to the Holy City and set him on
the parapet of the temple. 'If you are the Son of God', he
said, 'throw yourself down; for scripture says, "He will
put his angels in charge of you, and they will support you
in their arms, for fear you should strike your foot against
a stone."' Jesus answered him, 'Scripture also says, "You
are not to put the Lord your God to the test."'

Reading The second temptation today.

People today often want God to do what Jesus refused to
do, to compel them to believe in him. 'If there is a good
God, why doesn't he stop wars?' shouts one man, angrily.
'How can there be a God with all the evil there is in the
world?' demands somebody else. 'Why do I always lose
when I try to prove the existence of God to that atheist at
work?' asks a puzzled and shaken young Christian.

We want God to act, to establish himself as God, and
no nonsense! As someone once wrote, 'If I were God, I'd
at least have a brass plate on the door. Further, I'd get a
move on, I'd lay about me. If I were on the throne I'd
make some people's ears burn with boxing for their
persistent neglect.'

But this is not God's way. Our humanity is in our
freedom. If that is taken away we are persons no longer,

but just puppets on a string. Even God's very existence must be open to doubt to safeguard our personhood. If God established himself so compellingly that nobody could possibly doubt him, our ability to make a free response to him would be gone forever, and with it our humanity as well.

In the same way, it is a bigger thing that we should learn, however painfully, that war is wrong, than that God should step in and stop us fighting. God wants the love of sons and daughters who freely turn to him. But, meanwhile, there is no pain which he does not share. He is involved in the suffering of all his children. Jesus taught us this is not just by words, but by his own suffering and crucifixion.

PICTURE • PONDER • PRAY • PROMISE

Praise God who can do all things.

Pray for the churches, that they may seek to draw others
    to God by
    the love and the suffering of the risen Jesus
    for those tempted to cheapen the gospel by slick
        and theatrical devices.

A PRAYER

Lord of wonders, healings and miracles,
May our lives in your service
    draw others by our love for you. Amen.

Son of God, who learned obedience through suffering:
Keep us firm in faith when we are tested.
Son of God, made perfect through trial and
    temptation:
Keep us in the truth: your word is truth.

The second reading is from *To Me Personally* by Wilf Wilkinson, 1972, HarperCollins Publishers. London. Reproduced by permission.

THE TEMPTATIONS OF JESUS (3)

The third of three reflections on the temptations of Jesus as told in St Matthew's Gospel

The temptations of power by evil means

Father Creator:
Jesus Redeemer,
Spirit of truth:
We praise you for ever.

READING MATTHEW 4:8-10. R.E.B.
THE THIRD TEMPTATION OF CHRIST

The devil took him next to a very high mountain, and showed him all the kingdoms of the world in their glory. 'All these,' he said, 'I will give you, if you will only fall down and do me homage.' But Jesus said, 'Out of my sight, Satan! Scripture says, "You shall do homage to the Lord your God and worship him alone."'

READING THE THIRD TEMPTATION TODAY

Here is the temptation of some of our best people in politics and the social services – to make the building of a Welfare State, a just society, the complete and final aim. And here is the temptation of each one of us personally – to make our family, our work, some other good thing, our ultimate concern. If we make anything or anyone other than God our ultimate concern, we make it into an idol. God is the only true end. He, and he alone, must be our final aim. Normally, we serve God by loving our family and serving society. But we must love and serve them in God and for God, and should the situation ever arise when we have to choose between them and God, then we must say with Christ, 'You shall do homage to the Lord your God and worship him alone'.

One thing that fascinates me about this temptation is Jesus's attitude to authority. He will not exercise any authority which comes from an office or position. He says simply, 'I have come to bear witness to the truth. That is the only authority I have or want to have, I speak the truth.'

How relevant this is to our present 'Crises in authority'! To be a parson or teacher, parent or boss, no longer carries the authority it once did. Older people tend to bemoan the change and feel that things are going to the dogs. But isn't the only real authority the authority of truth, not position? Dare we be stripped of all power but that? If we dare, we be shall be very close to that wonderful Man of Nazareth.

PICTURE • PONDER • PRAY • PROMISE

Praise God for the incorruptibility of Jesus.

Pray for all in positions of trust, especially those whose opportunities for deception and corruption are very tempting.

A PRAYER

Lord Jesus Christ, you were tempted in every way,
    as we are:
You remained faithful,
    grant that we may do so, by your grace and love.
    Amen.

Son of God, who learned obedience through
    suffering:
Keep us firm in faith when we are tested.
Son of God, made perfect through trial and
    temptation:
Keep us in the truth: your word is truth.

The second reading is from *To Me Personally* by Wilf Wilkinson, 1972, HarperCollins Publishers, London. Reproduced by permission.

THE CALVARY TRIUMPH

*A reflection on how secular defeat became
eternal victory, and the cross, a throne of God*

Who shall ascend the hill of the Lord?
Or who shall stand in his holy place?
He that has clean hands and a pure heart:
Who has not set his soul upon idols,
nor sworn his oath to a lie:
He shall receive blessing from the Lord,
And recompense from the God of his salvation:
Who is the King of Glory?
The Lord of hosts, he is the King of glory.

READING MARK 15:25-39. R.E.B.
THE CENTURION SEES JESUS DIE

It was nine in the morning when they crucified him; and
the inscription giving the charge against him read, 'The
King of the Jews'. Two robbers were crucified with him,
one on his right and the other on his left.

The passers-by wagged their heads and jeered at him:
'Bravo!' they cried, 'So you are the man who was to pull
down the temple, and rebuild it in three days! Save
yourself and come down from the cross.' The chief priests
and scribes joined in, jesting with one another: 'He saved
others,' they said, 'but he cannot save himself. Let the
Messiah, the king of Israel, come down now from the
cross. If we see that, we shall believe.' Even those who
were crucified with him taunted him.

At midday a darkness fell over the whole land, which
lasted till three in the afternoon; and at three Jesus cried
aloud, 'Eloi, Eloi, lema sabachthani?' which means, 'My
God, my God, why have you forsaken me?' Hearing this,
some of the bystanders said, 'Listen! He is calling Elijah.'
Someone ran and soaked a sponge in sour wine and held
it to his lips on the end of a stick. 'Let us see', he said, 'if
Elijah will come to take him down.' Then Jesus gave a

loud cry and died; and the curtain of the temple was torn in two from top to bottom. When the centurion who was standing opposite him saw how he died, he said, 'This man must have been a son of God.'

READING 'THE DEATH OF JESUS THE CHRIST'

Procula	Centurion, were you at the killing of that teacher today?
Longinus	Yes, lady.
Procula	Tell me about his death.
Longinus	It is hardly fit hearing for you, my lady . . .
Procula	Do not tell it all then, but tell me what he said.
Longinus	The people were mocking him at first, and he prayed God to forgive them. He said, 'Father forgive them, for they know not what they do.'
Procula	Was he suffering much?
Longinus	No lady; he wasn't a strong man. The scourging must have nearly killed him. I thought he was dead by noon, and then suddenly he began to sing in a loud voice that he was giving back his spirit to God. I looked to see God come to take him. He died singing. Truly, lady, that man was the Son of God, if one may say that . . .
Procula	What do you think the man believed, centurion?
Longinus	He believed he was God, they say.
Procula	What do you think of that claim?
Longinus	If a man believes anything up to the point of dying on the cross for it, he will find others to believe it.
Procula	Do you believe it?
Longinus	He was a fine young fellow, my lady; not past middle age. And he was all alone and defied the Jews and all the Romans, and, when we had done with him, he was a poor broken-down thing, dead on the cross.

Procula   Do you think he is dead?

Longinus   No, lady, I don't.

Procula   Then where is he?

Longinus   Let loose in the world, lady, where neither
            Roman nor Jew can stop his truth.

PICTURE • PONDER • PRAY • PROMISE

Praise God for the life, death and resurrection of Jesus
  for the total victory which seemed total defeat
  for the patience under suffering of our Lord
  for the turning upside down of the world's expectations
  for all who have suffered triumphantly for Jesus
  for the hope of life that lasts eternally.

Pray for all who suffer unjustly
  for all who make other people suffer
  for the grace and strength to follow the way of Jesus.

Christ is risen:
He is risen indeed!
He lives in us now:
In his name we live for ever!

The opening response is Psalm 24:3,4,5 & 10.

The second reading is from *The Trial of Jesus* by John Masefield. Reproduced by permission of the Society of Authors as the literary representative of the Estate of John Masefield.

THE HOLY GHOST WITHIN

Divine fulfilment and human emptiness

Blessed be the God and Father of our Lord
  Jesus Christ!
By his great mercy,
We have been born anew to a living hope:
**Through the resurrection of Jesus Christ from
the dead.**

READING 'THE YOUNG MAN': A POEM OF THE 1930'S

There is this young man,
who lives in the world of progress.
He used to worship a God,
Who was kind to him.
The God had a long white beard,
He lived in the clouds,
but all the same,
He was close to the solemn child,
who had secretly
shut Him up, in a picture book.

But now,
the man is enlightened.
Now he has been to school,
and has learnt to kick a ball,
and to be abject
in the face of public opinion.
He knows, too,
that men are hardly removed from monkeys.
You see, he lives in the light
of the twentieth century.

He works twelve hours a day
and is able to rent a room,
in a lodging house that is not a home.
At night he hangs a wretched coat
up on a peg on a door

and stares at an awful jug and basin
and goes to bed.
And the poor coat,
worn to the man's shape,
round-shouldered and abject,
watches him asleep,
dreaming of all the essential, holy things,
that he cannot hope to obtain
from two pounds ten a week.

Very soon, he will put off his body,
like the poor dejected coat
that he hates.
And his body will be worn to the shape
of twelve hours work a day,
for two pounds ten a week.

If he had only known,
that the God in the picture book,
is not an old man in the clouds,
but the seed of life in his soul,
the man would have lived.
And his life would have flowered,
with the flower of limitless joy.

But he does not know,
and in him
the Holy Ghost,
is a poor little bird in a cage,
who never sings,
and never opens his wings,
yet never, never
desires to be gone away.

READING EPHESIANS 1:3-10. T.E.V.

Let us give thanks to the God and Father of our Lord Jesus
Christ! For in our union with Christ he has blessed us by
giving us every spiritual blessing in the heavenly world.
Even before the world was made, God had already chosen

us to be his through our union with Christ, so that we would be holy and without fault before him.

Because of his love God had already decided that through Jesus Christ he would make us his sons – this was his pleasure and purpose. Let us praise God for his glorious grace, for the free gift he gave us in his dear Son! For by the sacrificial death of Christ we are set free, that is, our sins are forgiven. How great is the grace of God, which he gave to us in such large measure!

In all his wisdom and insight God did what he had purposed, and made known to us the secret plan he had already decided to complete by means of Christ. This plan, which God will complete when the time is right, is to bring all creation together, everything in heaven and on earth, with Christ as head.

PICTURE · PONDER · PRAY · PROMISE

Lord God, Creator, Saviour, Spirit:
We thank you for love freely given,
We praise you for a destiny far beyond our
     deserving:
Open us in heart and mind,
Break down the limits of our faltering faith:
And make us wholly yours. Amen.

The first reading is from *The Flowering Tree*, by Caryll Houselander, Sheed & Ward. Reproduced by permission.

LOVE AND WAR

The suffering and evil of warfare; for Remembrancetide

To bind all things together:
There must be love.
Let the peace of Christ:
Rule in our hearts.

READING 1 JOHN 4:7-12. J.B.
LIFE AS IT CAN BECOME IN CHRIST

My dear people,
let us love one another
since love comes from God
and everyone who loves is begotten by God
    and knows God.
Anyone who fails to love can never have known God
because God is love.
God's love for us was revealed
when God sent into the world his only Son
so that we could have life through him;
this is the love I mean:
not our love for God,
but God's love for us when he sent his Son
to be the sacrifice that takes our sins away.
My dear people,
since God has loved us so much,
we too should love one another.
No one has ever seen God;
but as long as we love one another
God will live in us
and his love will be complete in us.

READING GHOSTS, FIRE AND WATER – A POEM INSPIRED
BY THE HIROSHIMA MEMORIAL PANEL

These are the ghosts of the unwilling dead.
Grey ghosts of that imprinted flash of memory
Whose flaming and eternal instant haunts
The speechless dark with dread and anger.

Grey, out of pale nothingness their agony appears,
Like ash they are blown and blasted on the wind's
Vermilion breathlessness, like shapeless smoke
Their shapes are torn across the paper sky.

These scarred and ashen ghosts are quick
With Pain's unutterable speech, their flame-cracked flesh
Writhes and is heavy as the worm's, the bitter dirt;
Lonely as in death they bleed, naked as in birth.

They greet each other in a ghastly paradise,
These ghosts who cannot come with gifts and flowers.
Here they receive each other with disaster's common love,
Covering one another's pain with shrivelled hands.

They are not beautiful, yet beauty is in their truth.
There is no easy music in their silent screams,
No ordered dancing in their grief's distracted limbs.
Their shame is ours. We, too, are haunted by their fate.

In the shock of flame, their tears brand our flesh,
We twist in their agony and our scorching throats
Parch for the waters where the cool dead float.
We press our lips upon the river where they drink, and
    drown.

Their voices call us, in pain and indignation:
'This is what you have done to us!'
– Their accusation is our final hope, Be comforted.
Yes, we have heard you, ghosts of our indifference.

We hear your cry, we understand your warnings.
We, too, shall refuse to accept our fate!
Haunt us with the truth of our betrayal
Until the earth's united voices shout refusal,
    sing your peace!

Forgive us, that we had to see your passion to remember
What we must never again deny: LOVE ONE ANOTHER.

PICTURE · PONDER · PRAY · PROMISE

Creator God, may the waste and the foolishness
of war:
Cease throughout your world.
Saviour God, may mankind learn to love and
forgive:
and to live in the ways of fellowship.
Guiding God, grant wisdom and the love of peace:
to all who wield power in your world.
Centre our hopes on you:
for you are the hope of the world.

The second reading is from *The Descent Into the Cave* (1957) by James Kirkup, published by Oxford University Press. Reproduced by permission of the author.

TRUE WISDOM

Holy Wisdom is more than factual knowledge

O Lord, open our lips:
To praise you with wisdom and love.
The fear of the Lord:
Is the beginning of knowledge.
Whoever finds wisdom finds life:
Let us hear and be wise.

READING PROVERBS 8:22-31. R.S.V.

Wisdom speaks:

The Lord created me at the beginning of his work,
    the first of his acts of old.
Ages ago I was set up,
    at the first, before the beginning of the earth.
When there were no depths I was brought forth,
    when there were no springs abounding with water.
Before the mountains had been shaped,
    before the hills, I was brought forth;
before he had made the earth with its fields,
    or the first of the dust of the world.
When he established the heavens, I was there,
    when he drew a circle on the face of the deep,
when he made firm the skies above,
    when he established the fountains of the deep,
when he assigned to the sea its limit,
    so that the waters might not transgress his command,
when he marked out the foundations of the earth,
    then I was beside him, like a master workman;
and I was daily his delight,
    rejoicing before him always,
rejoicing in his inhabited world
    and delighting in the sons of men.

READING 'KNOWLEDGE AND WISDOM' – WORDS OF A. N. WHITEHEAD

We must take it as unavoidable that God has so made the world that there are more topics desirable for knowledge than any one person can possibly acquire. It is hopeless to approach the problem by the way of the enumeration of subjects which everyone ought to have mastered. There are too many of them, all with excellent title-deeds. Perhaps, after all, this plethora of material is fortunate; for the world is made interesting by a delightful ignorance of important truths. What I am anxious to impress on you is that though knowledge is one chief aim of intellectual education, there is another ingredient, vaguer but greater, and more dominating in its importance. The ancients called it 'wisdom'. You cannot be wise without some basis of knowledge; but you may easily acquire knowledge and remain bare of wisdom.

Now wisdom is the way in which knowledge is held. It concerns the handling of knowledge . . . The only avenue towards wisdom is by freedom in the presence of knowledge.

PICTURE • PONDER • PRAY • PROMISE

A PRAYER

Almighty God,
give us wisdom to perceive you,
intellect to understand you,
diligence to seek you,
patience to wait for you,
vision to discern you,
a heart to meditate upon you,
and life to proclaim your glory. Amen.

Thank God for learning and for wisdom to use our
  learning well.

Pray for all who teach
  for all who learn,
  for those deprived of the learning they need to use
    their gifts of hand and brain.

Lord Jesus, revealer of truth:
Lead us into a love of true learning.
Lord Jesus, master of the art of living:
Show us how to live wisely.
Lord Jesus, eternal Saviour:
We live by your grace.

The second reading is from *The Aims of Education* by A. N. Whitehead,
published by Williams & Norgate, 1932.

CHRISTIAN ANGER

Divine indignation and human rage:
a reflection and a contrast

O Lord, open our lips:
To praise you, creator and king.
You are just in all your judgements:
And true in all your ways.

READING MATTHEW 21:12-17. T.E.V
TWO SORTS OF ANGER

Jesus went into the Temple and drove out all those who were buying and selling there. He overturned the tables of the money-changers and the stools of those who sold pigeons, and said to them, 'It is written in the Scriptures that God said, "My Temple will be called a house of prayer." But you are making it a hideout for thieves!'

The blind and the crippled came to him in the Temple, and he healed them. The chief priests and the teachers of the Law became angry when they saw the wonderful things he was doing and the children shouting in the Temple, 'Praise to David's Son!' So they asked Jesus, 'Do you hear that they are saying?'

'Indeed I do,' answered Jesus. 'Haven't you ever read this scripture? "You have trained children and babies to offer perfect praise."'

Jesus left them and went out of the city to Bethany, where he spent the night.

READING 'CRUCIFIED DAILY': AN ANGRY POEM

What is it like, Lord, to die
In pain on Calvary's hill,
And know that those who condemn you
Thought they were doing God's will?

What is it like, Lord, to walk
Through streets where no-one cares,
And seeing the people all passing,
Wrapped up in private affairs?

What is it like, Lord, to starve,
With barren fields all round,
And know that somewhere else, farmers
Plough food back into the ground?

What is it like, Lord, to bleed
In a war's consuming flame,
And know that those who hate you
Hate you in liberty's name.

What is like, Lord, to die
In pain each day again?
For still you're crucified daily,
Living and dying with men.

PICTURE · PONDER · PRAY · PROMISE

A Prayer

Father, Son, Spirit, teach us the anger
that grows from love and compassion.
Cleanse us from all other rage, bitterness and spite.
Amen.

Praise God that there is a true outlet for human anger
and indignation.

Pray to share the divine point of view and God's
discernment of what is good and is evil.
Pray to be like Jesus.
Pray that your own anger and wrath may be made holy.

Come then and see what the Lord has done:
What destruction he has brought upon the earth.
He makes wars to cease in all he world:
He breaks the bow and shatters the spear.
He turns the wrath of mankind:
Into thirst for justice.

The second reading is by Peter Casey (date and publisher unknown).
The first four lines of the final response are from Psalm 46:8-9a.

OPEN-HEARTEDNESS

Traditional religion under examination

Father, we adore you:
We are here to be open to your love.
Christ, we adore you:
We come to you for enlightenment.
Spirit, we adore you:
We live and have being in your truth.
Holy Trinity – three persons in one:
We love you, since you love us always.

READING MATTHEW 15:1-9. T.E.V.
SPIRITUAL INSIGHT AND THE POWER OF
FAMILIAR IDEAS

Some Pharisees and teachers of the Law came from Jerusalem to Jesus and asked him, 'Why is it that your disciples disobey the teaching handed down by our ancestors? They don't wash their hands in the proper way before they eat!'

Jesus answered, 'And why do you disobey God's command and follow your own teaching? For God said, "Respect your father and your mother," and, "Whoever curses his father or his mother is to be put to death." But you teach that if a person has something he could use to help his father or mother, but says, "This belongs to God," he does not need to honour his father. In this way you disregard God's command, in order to follow your own teaching. You hypocrites! How right Isaiah was when he prophesied about you!

"These people, says God, honour me with their words, but their heart is really far away from me.

It is no use for them to worship me, because they teach man-made rules as though they were my laws!"'

READING ON CLOSED-HEARTEDNESS

People reveal themselves by what they notice and what they say . . . The Pharisees of Jesus's day noticed – what? The miracles of healing? Sturdy fishermen and tax collectors finding religion as a force that made them give up their jobs and work together? The personality of Jesus? Their own false values and ineffectiveness? No, none of these things. They noticed what they were looking for, 'that some of His disciples ate their food with "common" (that is, unwashed) hands.' Their hearts were closed.

PICTURE • PONDER • PRAY • PROMISE

A PRAYER

> Lord God, loving Father,
> Help us to open before you every thought and
>   secret within us.
> That gaining insight in our need for mercy,
> We may gain your blessing and forgiveness,
> And learn to see life with the eyes of Christ. Amen.

> Pray to repent, sincerely, deeply, fully:

> Praise God that he loves and forgives us all.

> Pray for those gripped by evil, greed, addiction,
>   bitterness of heart:

> Praise God that he can break the chains of evil
>   and the power of sin.

> Lord, may we honour you in word:
> **And be close to you in our hearts.**
> May we worship you:
> **In spirit and in truth.**

The second reading is from *Letters to Parsi* by Roger Hicks, 1967, Blandford Press.

THE FULL LIFE

*A reflection on the words of Jesus in the Gospel of
St John: 'I have come that they may have life,
and may have it in all its fulness'*

Open our lips, O Lord:
To praise your holy name.
Open our lives, O Lord:
To live your holy life.
Open our memories and minds:
To be rooted in your love.

READING 1 CORINTHIANS 13. R.E.B.
LOVE, THE CLUE TO FULNESS OF LIFE

I may speak in tongues of men or of angels, but if I have
no love, I am a sounding gong or a clanging cymbal. I
may have the gift of prophecy and the knowledge of
every hidden truth; I may have faith enough to move
mountains; but if I have no love, I am nothing. I may give
all I possess to the needy, I may give my body to be burnt,
but if I have no love, I gain nothing by it.

Love is patient and kind. Love envies no one, is never
boastful, never conceited, never rude; love is never selfish,
never quick to take offence. Love keeps no score of
wrongs, takes no pleasure in the sins of others, but
delights in the truth. There is nothing love cannot face;
there is no limit to its faith, its hope, its endurance.

Love will never come to an end. Prophecies will cease;
tongues of ecstasy will fall silent; knowledge will vanish.
For our knowledge and our prophecy alike are partial,
and the partial vanishes when wholeness comes. When I
was a child I spoke like a child, thought like a child,
reasoned like a child; but when I grew up I finished with
childish things. At present we see only puzzling
reflections in a mirror, but one day we shall see face to
face. My knowledge now is partial; then it will be whole,
like God's knowledge of me. There are three things that

last for ever: faith, hope, and love; and the greatest of the three is love.

READING LOVE AND DIVINE CHARITY BRING FULNESS OF LIVING

It is because religion in the true sense is as comprehensive as life itself that we cannot find God or serve Him or love Him with a mere part of ourselves – let us say, by a mere effort of will, by gritting the teeth and clenching the fist. What we most truly are in the depths of our being refuses to surrender to force – force from within no more than force from without. That is what St Augustine meant when he said that Christ's command to love God is not obeyed if it is obeyed as a command. That is what St. Paul meant when he said, 'Though I bestow all my goods to feed the poor, and though I give my body to be burned, and have not charity, it profiteth me nothing.'

Nor can we find Him in whom we live and move and have our being simply by the exercise of our intelligence. You will remember in Hans Anderson's story of the Snow Queen, how little Kay with the ice-blocks of reason could never find out how to place them in order to form a word he was most anxious to make, – the word 'Eternity'. The fact is that although the claims of the intellect are pretentious, its bag is disappointing. It has to kill the living reality before it can make it its own. 'Though' is always a post-mortem. That was what St Paul meant when he said, 'Though I . . . understand all mysteries . . . and all knowledge . . . and have not charity, I am nothing.'

Nor can we find God merely by being religious in the narrow, technical sense. Eight hundred years before Christ, the prophets of Israel proclaimed this fact when they condemned as useless the religious ritual of their day. But ritual need not be external. It can take the form of devotional cliches, or the manipulating of people so as to produce in them a certain type of psychological experience. Religion, in this sense, is not enough. For 'Though I speak with the tongues of men and of angels . . . though I have the gift of prophecy . . . though I have all faith, so that I could remove mountains, and have not charity, I am nothing.'

Charity is not consequence. It is not reward. Charity is gift, God's gift of himself to us, the gift which makes us what we are. And we do not receive it in any specialised activity abstracted from the rest of our lives, for God gives Himself to us in everything, including our own nature. In our own capacity to feel, to think, to criticise, to condemn, to love, to resolve, to endure – there is God giving Himself to us, there is that most excellent gift of charity.

Charity is the power to accept, to accept ourselves and other people and the world as the presence of God. Charity is the power not to deny but to affirm experience, not to shrink away from it in frozen or indignant alarm but to go out and meet it, because, in spite of the apparent threats and dangers, it is our creator, come, not to steal, nor to kill, nor to destroy, but that we might have life and have it more abundantly.

PICTURE • PONDER • PRAY • PROMISE

A PRAYER

Lord, you have taught us
that all our doings without love are worth nothing.
Send your Holy Spirit
and pour into our hearts that most excellent gift of love,
the true bond of peace and of all virtues,
without which whoever lives is counted dead
before you.
Grant this for the sake of your only Son,
Jesus Christ our Lord. Amen.

Thank God for his love.

Reflect on and enjoy his love for you, however difficult you
find it to love yourself.

Pray for the grace to love others, however hard you find it
to love them.

Pray for those who feel they have no-one to love them,
here or in heaven.

> There are three things that last for ever:
> **Faith, hope and love;**
> And the greatest of the three:
> **Is love. Alleluia!**

The opening words of this order for worship are from John 10:10. R.E.B.

The second reading is from *The True Wilderness*, by H. A. Williams, 1965,
Constable Publishers. Reproduced by permission.

The final response is from I Corinthians 13:13. R.E.B.

Nothing Shall Separate Us

The misery of despair confronts the love of God

Blessed be God:
The Father our Lord Jesus Christ.
Blessed be God:
Who gives new birth.
Blessed be God:
Who raised Jesus Christ from the dead.
Blessed be God:
For our hope and our promise of heaven.

READING 'THE HOUSE OF THE RISING SUN':
A PROSTITUTE'S LAMENT

There is a house in New Orleans
They call it the Rising Sun,
And it's been the ruin of many poor girls,
And me, O God, for one.

If I had listened to what my mother said,
I'd have been at home today,
But I was young and foolish, O God,
Let rambling lead me astray.

Go, tell my baby sister,
'Don't do what I have done,
But shun that house in New Orleans,
They call it the Rising Sun.'

I'm going back to New Orleans,
My race is almost run,
I'm going back to spend my life,
Beneath that Rising Sun.

READING ROMANS 8:26-39. J.B. GOD'S LOVE IN ACTION

The Spirit too comes to help us in our weakness. For when we cannot choose words in order to pray properly, the Spirit himself expresses our plea in a way that could never be put into words, and God who knows everything in our hearts knows perfectly well what he means, and that the pleas of the saints expressed by the Spirit are according to the mind of God.

We know that by turning everything to their good God co-operates with all those who love him, with all those that he has called according to his purpose. They are the ones he chose specially long ago and intended to become true images of his Son, so that his Son might be the eldest of many brothers. He called those he intended for this; those he called he justified, and with those he justified he shared his glory.

After saying this, what can we add? With God on our side who can be against us? Since God did not spare his own Son, but gave him up to benefit us all, we may be certain, after such a gift, that he will not refuse anything he can give. Could anyone accuse those that God has chosen?

When God acquits, could anyone condemn? Could Christ Jesus? No! He not only died for us – he rose from the dead, and there at God's right hand he stands and pleads for us.

Nothing therefore can come between us and the love of Christ, even if we are troubled or worried, or being persecuted, or lacking food or clothes, or being threatened or even attacked. As scripture promised: *For your sake we are being massacred daily, and reckoned as sheep for the slaughter*. These are the trials through which we triumph, by the power of him who loved us.

For I am certain of this: neither death nor life, no angel, no prince, nothing that exists, nothing still to come, not any power, or height or depth, nor any created thing, can ever come between us and the love of God made visible in Christ Jesus our Lord.

PICTURE • PONDER • PRAY • PROMISE

Thank God for his love
   the heart of creation
   the heart of salvation
   the heart of the Spirit of life.

Pray for all who have lost self-respect and hope
   prostitutes and those who use them,
   drug addicts and those who supply them,
   those tempted to suicide and despair,
   thieves and compulsive gamblers,
   the over-anxious and afraid,
   those who know no-one who shows them love.

A PRAYER

Give us, O Lord, so strong a sense of your mercy
   and kindness
that we may gladly put our trust in you for ever.
   Amen.

God knows all things well:
And our prayers come before him.
He is our hope:
And the hope of all creation.

The words of the first reading are from a traditional N. American folk Song.

The opening response is based on I Peter 1:3,4,. J.B.

THE TRANSFORMING POWER OF LOVE

*A reflection on the central truth
of faith: God's love*

O Lord, open our lips:
To proclaim your love and your grace.
Let us worship you, Lord:
And live in the peace of our faith.

READING LUKE 6:36-50. T.E.V.

'Be merciful just as your Father is merciful.

Do not judge others, and God will not judge you; do not condemn others, and God will not condemn you; forgive others, and God will forgive you. Give to others, and God will give to you. Indeed, you will receive a full measure, a generous helping, poured into your hands – all that you can hold. The measure you use for others is the one that God will use for you.'

And Jesus told them this parable: 'One blind man cannot lead another one; if he does, both will fall into a ditch. No pupil is greater than his teacher; but every pupil, when has has completed his training, will be like his teacher.

Why do you look at the speck in your brother's eye, but pay no attention to the log in your own eye? How can you say to your brother, "Please, brother, let me take that speck out of your eye," yet cannot even see the log in your own eye? You hypocrite! First take the log out of your own eye, and then you will be able to see clearly to take the speck out of your brother's eye.

A healthy tree does not bear bad fruit, nor does a poor tree bear good fruit. Every tree is know by the fruit it bears; you do not pick figs from thorn bushes or gather grapes from bramble bushes. A good person brings good out of the treasure of good things in his heart; a bad person brings bad out of his treasure of bad things. For the mouth speaks what the heart is full of.

Why do you call me, "Lord, Lord", and yet don't do what I tell you? Anyone who comes to me and listens to my words and obeys them – I will show you what he is like. He is like a man who, in building his house, dug deep and laid the foundation on rock. The river overflowed and hit that house but could not shake it, because it was well built. But anyone who hears my words and does not obey them is like a man who built his house without laying a foundation; when the flood hit that house it fell at once – and what a terrible crash that was!'

READING EVIL TRANSFORMED BY LOVE

'Love! Love!' said St Francis, 'Not war, not force! Even prayer, brother, is not enough; good works are needed too. It is difficult and dangerous to live among men, but necessary. To withdraw into the wilderness and pray is too easy, too convenient. . . . Wherever you find men, you will also find suffering, illness and sin. That is where our place is, my brother; with the lepers, sinners and with those who are starving. Deep down in the bowels of every man, even the saintliest ascetic, there sleeps a horrible larva. Lean over and say to this larva: "I love you!" and it will sprout wings and become a butterfly.'

PICTURE • PONDER • PRAY • PROMISE

Praise God for his love and its power to transform us

Pray for the church and for all Christians, that we may have the gift of love.

God of love:
Teach us to love.
God of mercy and forgiveness:
Teach us to forgive.
God of grace and renewing power:
Teach us to look for the good in others.
God of strength:
Teach us to persist in loving.
For Jesus's sake:
Amen.

The second reading is from *St Francis* by Nikos Kazantzakis.

THE AWFUL DEMANDS
OF LOVING

*A reflection that all human beings are one
in their need for compassion*

O Lord, open our lips:
To rejoice in your strength and your love.
Let us praise the God who saves us:
And who frees us from evil and death.

READING ISAIAH 53: 1-6. R.E.B.
CHRIST'S SUFFERING IS FORETOLD

Who could have believed what we have heard?
To whom has the power of the Lord been revealed?

He grew up before the Lord like a young plant
whose roots are in parched ground;
he had no beauty, no majesty to catch our eyes,
no grace to attract us to him.
He was despised, shunned by all,
pain-racked and afflicted by disease;
we despised him, we held him of no account,
an object from which people turn away their eyes.

Yet it was our afflictions he was bearing,
our pain he endured,
while we thought of him as smitten by God,
struck down by disease and misery.

But he was pierced for our transgressions,
crushed for our iniquities;
the chastisement he bore restored us to health
and by his wounds we are healed.

We had all strayed like sheep,
each of us going his own way,
the Lord laid on him
the guilt of us all.

READING TO HAVE TRUE COMPASSION FOR OTHERS,
     WE MUST SUFFER CRUCIFIXION WITH CHRIST

Suppose we come across a kleptomaniac. We may be enlightened enough to realise that simply to condemn him as a criminal does no good to anybody. Instead we may think of him and behave towards him as somebody who has a disease called kleptomania, like a man who has measles. But this apparently enlightened, clinical approach is in fact an attempt to prevent ourselves from perceiving how much we have in common with him. For his stealing is an attempt to compensate himself for an intolerable sense of having no value, and this sense of having no value follows from his never having been properly loved.

Now none of us has been fully loved. It is true of all of us that in this way or that way to this degree or that degree, the love we needed to feel our own value has been withheld. And so the spectre of valuelessness haunts us all, waiting to spring. And quite a lot of the things I do are attempts to avert my gaze from this ghost who would take from me all reasons for living. True, my own way of compensating myself for the threatening sense of valuelessness is not that of the kleptomaniac. I do not go around shop-lifting. But I see to it none the less, that I accumulate quite a lot of riches: I'm a good sort, I have friends who like me, I get a First in the Tripos, I have a strong will, I went to an expensive school, I have working-class parents, I have a girl-friend who is acknowledged to be exceedingly pretty, I have had a lot of sex, I am a pillar of the college chapel, I am a man of prayer and people realise that I live close to God.

Now all this sort of riches builds up an impenetrable barrier between myself and the kleptomaniac. For what he needs is somebody who will relinquish these mirages and brave the appalling desert of valuelessness, where he and I both in fact really are. It is in the acknowledgement of this common bond, in the realisation that he and I are in the same hell, that true compassion is born and grows. It is not that I am healthy and he is diseased. Both of us suffer from the same wounds, and that is how we can meet and communicate with each other.

'There but for the grace of God, go I' sounds pious, but it speaks not of compassion but of superiority. Compassion says 'There, by the grace of God, I have been and am.' It is in this sense surely that we should understand St Paul's words about Jesus: that 'God made Him to be sin for us, Who knew no sin', or St Matthew's words, echoing Isaiah, 'Himself took our infirmities, and bare our sickness.' 'Christ,' said Calvin, 'endured in his soul the dreadful torments of a condemned and lost man.' The reason why we fail in compassion is because we are too frightened thus to follow Jesus to the cross, going forth unto him bearing His reproach, filling up our share in His affliction . . .

This is the great and glorious paradox of Christian experience – that it is by dying that we live, that it is by sharing with Jesus the horror of His agony that we live with Him reigning indestructibly in peace.

PICTURE • PONDER • PRAY • PROMISE

A PRAYER

Lord, help us to share your cross in our lives,
that we may show clearly your life and your love.
Amen.

Christ bore our afflictions:
Enduring our pain.
His suffering, our healing:
His wounds are our hope.
Lord, teach us to live:
By what we believe. Amen.

The second reading is from Sermon 14 of *The True Wilderness* by H. A. Williams 1965, Constable Publishers. Reproduced by permission.

ACCEPTING DESTINY

A reflection on daily discipleship

WORDS OF KAHLIL GIBRAN

God has placed a torch in your hearts that glows with knowledge and beauty; it is a sin to extinguish that torch and bury it in the ashes.

> O Lord, the giver of each day:
> **Open our minds to your reality.**
> O Lord, ruler of space and time:
> **We praise your infinite glory.**

READING JEREMIAH 1:4-10. T.E.V.
A CALL TO BE ACTIVE FOR GOD

The Lord said to me, 'I chose you before I gave you life, and before you were born I selected you to be a prophet to the nations.'

I answered, 'Sovereign Lord, I don't know how to speak; I am too young.'

But the Lord said to me, 'Do not say that you are too young, but go to the people I send you to, and tell them everything I command you to say. Do not be afraid of them, for I will be with you to protect you. I, the Lord, have spoken!'

Then the Lord stretched out his hand, touched my lips, and said to me, 'Listen, I am giving you the words you must speak. Today I give you authority over nations and kingdoms to uproot and to pull down, to destroy and to overthrow, to build and to plant.'

READING KICKING AT DESTINY

Not only those who suffer cruelly, like Christ, but all of us, however soft our circumstances to an outward eye, kick at the destiny to which we are tied, and wriggle on the nails of our easy crucifixion. 'If only I were someone else – if I were untied from this difficult marriage – if I were released from this routine – if I could be free from anxiety – if my health did not cramp my spirits – if only . . . then,' we say, not merely, which is obvious, 'I should be more comfortable,' but, 'then I could begin to do something, instead of merely existing; then,' we may even dare to say, 'I could do something for God.' This is the great deception of the devil, to stop us loving, praying, working, now. It may be God's will that you should fight your way out of your misfortunes; it cannot be his will that you should make them a reason to put off living as a child of God.

PICTURE • PONDER • PRAY • PROMISE

A PRAYER

We thank you, Lord, for the gift of life;
   for health and strength, for limbs, and brains,
   for all our natural powers:
Help us use them aright.

We thank you, Lord, for the gift of our senses;
   for seeing, hearing, and for speech:
Help us use them aright.

We thank you, Lord, for our minds;
   for thought and reasoning, for powers of decision:
Help us use them aright.

We thank you, Lord, for the ability to love and fall in love;
   for the gift of sex and the power to procreate:
Help us use them aright.

We thank you, Lord, for our sympathies; for being able to
   care and able to give cheerfulness and patience:
Help us use them aright.

We thank you, Lord, for gifts and talents; for excellence
   and genius given to individual men and women:
Help us use them aright. Amen.

Pray for people who can find no fulfilment of their gifts and abilities, out of fear or by the cruelty of others.

> Lord, we accept this day:
> **In all its reality.**
> Lord, help us to live:
> **In the way of Jesus. Amen.**

The second reading is from *Lord, I believe* by Austin Farrer, 1958, Faith Press.

Before You, Lord

A reflection on the simplicity of true prayer

Our Father in heaven:
Teach us to hallow your name.
Your kingdom shall come:
Teach us the silence of faith.

READING MATTHEW 6:5-8. T.E.V.
THE APPROACH TO PRAYER

When you pray, do not be like the hypocrites! They love to stand up and pray in the houses of worship and on the street corners, so that everyone will see them. I assure you, they have already been paid in full. But when you pray, go to your room, close the door, and pray to your Father, who is unseen. And your Father, who sees what you do in private, will reward you.

When you pray, do not use a lot of meaningless words, as the pagans do, who think that their gods will hear them because their prayers are long. Do not be like them. Your Father already knows what you need before you ask him.

READING A MEDITATION

To be there before you, Lord, that's all.
To shut the eyes of my body,
To shut the eyes of my soul,
And be still and silent,
To expose myself to you who are there, exposed to me.
To be there before you, the Eternal Presence.

I am willing to feel nothing, Lord
    to see nothing,
    to hear nothing.
Empty of all ideas,
    of all images,
In the darkness.
Here I am, simply,

To meet you without obstacles,
In the silence of faith,
Before you, Lord.

But, Lord, I am not alone
I can no longer be alone.
I am in a crowd, Lord,
For men live within me.
I have met them.
They have come in,
They have settled down,
They have worried me,
They have tormented me,
They have devoured me.
And I have allowed it, Lord, that they might be nourished
    and refreshed.
I bring them to you, too, as I come before you.
Here I am,
Here they are,
Before you, Lord.

PICTURE • PONDER • PRAY • PROMISE

Thank God for the gift of prayer.

Pray for simplicity in faith and prayer.

Pray for the calm and serenity to be silent before God
    to know more of his love and beauty.

Pray for those too busy
    too anxious,
    too fearful,
    too angry,
    too ill,
    too hungry,
    too wretched and guilty to pray.

A Prayer

Lord, do not make us ambitious to be good, successful,
   holy and great:
Help us to know your love,
And our need of peace with you. Amen.

The peace of God:
Is greater than we can understand.
In stillness and in quiet waiting:
God will perfect us.

The second reading is from *Prayers of Life*, by Michel Quoist, 1963, Gill and
MacMillan Publishers, Dublin. Reproduced by permission.

TWO CALLS TO REPENTANCE

Outbursts of holy anger

Glory to God in the highest:
And peace to his people on earth.
Lord God, heavenly King:
Almighty God, and Father,
We worship you:
We praise you for your glory.

READING FALSE RELIGION

Glory to man in the highest,
For man is the maker of gadgets.
Hail to the Unholy
Who gives us –
That which we wish to get.

O thou who makest no demands
Who winkest the tolerant eye
At our adultery
And understandest our great need
To get rich quick,
We worship and adore thee.

This is the sort of God we like.
This is the sort of God we can worship
His face is our face.
Because we made his face in our image.

But from this other –
From this God who is a person,
Breaking and entering our lives.
From this God who meddles
With details that do not concern him:
Passing judgement on habits of thought,
And speech,
Our practice in sex, sleep and labour,
Entering the innermost being.
From this meddling God,
From this interfering God,
Good Lord, deliver us!

READING MALACHI 2:17-3:5. R.E.B.

You have wearied the Lord with your talk. You ask, 'How have we wearied him?' By saying that all evildoers are good in the eyes of the Lord, that he is pleased with them, or by asking, 'Where is the God of justice?' I am about to send my messenger to clear a path before me. Suddenly the Lord whom you seek will come to his temple; the messenger of the covenant in whom you delight is here, here already, says the Lord of Hosts. Who can endure the day of his coming? Who can stand firm when he appears? He is like a refiner's fire, like a fuller's soap; he will take his seat, testing and purifying; he will purify the Levites and refine them like gold and silver, and so they will be fit to bring offerings to the Lord. Thus the offerings of Judah and Jerusalem will be pleasing to the Lord as they were in former days, in years long past. I shall appear before you in court, quick to testify against sorcerers, adulterers, and perjurers, against those who cheat the hired labourer of his wages, who wrong the widow and the fatherless, who thrust the alien aside and do not fear me, says the Lord of Hosts.

PICTURE • PONDER • PRAY • PROMISE

Reflecting on the stern words of the readings:

Praise God for his holiness, truth and insight
into human motives.

Pray for a sense of personal realism
liberation from self-deception,
the grace of repentance.

A PRAYER

All-holy God and Father of creation,
Expose for us the lies and self-deceptions of our
a hearts and minds:
And seeing ourselves in truth,
May we see your loving mercy,
Shown to us in Jesus Christ our Lord. Amen.

Day by day, dear Lord:
Of you three things we pray;
To see you more clearly:
To love you more dearly,
To follow you more nearly:
In Christ our Lord. Amen.

The opening response is from *Gloria in Excelsis Deo*, ASB translation.

The first reading is from *Christ in the Concrete City*, by P. W. Turner, 1956, SPCK. Reproduced by permission.

The final response is based on a prayer attributed to St Richard of Chichester.

PEOPLE!

A reflection on the unity of mankind in its creator

Creator God, Lord of heaven and earth:
From you is life and breath – we praise your name.
Father of being and time:
We are your children.
Open our lips to praise your name:
And fill our lives with your love.

READING THESE ARE PEOPLE!

I remember a time in my life when I hid with great care, behind high walls I erected between myself and reality. This meant that I had to keep human beings on the other side of the wall too, along with issues and threatening ideas. Then I realised one day that the walls were crumbling, very gradually, very slowly. I knew there would be no Jericho for me, no instantaneous collapse of the walls I had set up, no single great roar to be followed by clarity and relationship. But even then, as I peered out from behind the crumbling walls, as I had done many times before, for the first time I saw people instead of persons. It seems so important to me now that we see individuals instead of 'suburbanites', 'negroes' 'liberals', 'niggers', 'conservatives', 'wops', 'beatniks', 'Jews', 'labourites', 'kikes', 'Black Nationalists', 'white devils', 'moderates', 'radicals'. *These are people!*

READING EPHESIANS 3:14-21. T.E.V.

I fall on my knees before the Father, from whom every family in heaven and on earth receives its true name. I ask God from the wealth of his glory to give you power through his Spirit to be strong in your inner selves, and I pray that Christ will make his home in your hearts through faith. I pray that you may have your roots and foundation in love, so that you, together with all God's people, may have the power to understand how broad and long, how high and deep, is Christ's love. Yes, may you come to know his love – although it can never be fully known – and so be completely filled with the very nature of God.

To him who by means of his power working in us is able to do so much more than we can ever ask for, or even think of: to God be the glory in the church and in Christ Jesus for all time, for ever and ever! Amen.

PICTURE · PONDER · PRAY · PROMISE

Praise God for the unity, healing and maturity which
    Jesus offers to the human race.
Pray for the human race,
    for peace and mercy, forgiveness and respect between
      people
    for the finding of human perfection
    in Jesus our Lord.

A PRAYER

Lord God, you have made humanity to live
    as one family:
Teach us to respect the lives and hopes of others,
Teach us to rejoice in differences of colour,
    race, and origin,
Make us one in Christ. Amen.

    Christ himself is our peace:
    In him all are made one.
    Christ is the corner-stone:
    We are united in him.

The first reading is from *Book of Days*, by Malcolm Boyd, 1968, Heinemann Publishers (Oxford) Ltd. Reproduced by permission.

KINDRED AND AFFINITY

*God's life and love are not confused
by conventional religion*

O Lord, open our lips:
And fill our hearts with love.
O Lord, open our eyes:
With visions of your truth.
O Lord, broaden our minds:
And deepen our compassion.

READING AFFINITY

Consider this man in the field beneath,
Gaithered in mud, lost in his own breath,
Without joy, without sorrow,
without children, without wife,
Stumbling insensitively from furrow to furrow,
A vague somnambulist; but hold your tears,
For his name also is written in the Book of Life.

Ransack your brainbox, pull out the drawers
That rot in your heart's dust, and what have you to give
To enrich his spirit or the way he lives?
From the standpoint of education or caste or creed
Is there anything to show that your essential need
Is less than his, who has the world for church,
And stands bare-headed in the woods' wide porch
Morning and evening to hear God's choir
Scatter their praises? Don't be taken in
By stinking garments or an aimless grin;
He also is human, and the same small star,
That lights you homeward, has inflamed his mind
With the old hunger, born of his kind.

READING JOHN 10:14-18. T.E.V.

I am the good shepherd. As the Father knows me and I know the Father, in the same way I know my sheep and they know me. And I am willing to die for them. There are other sheep which belong to me that are not in this sheepfold. I must bring them, too; they will listen to my voice, and they will become one flock with one shepherd.

The Father loves me because I am willing to give up my life, in order that I may receive it back again. No one takes my life away from me. I give it up of my own free will. I have the right to give it up, and I have the right to take it back. This is what my Father has commanded me to do.

PICTURE • PONDER • PRAY • PROMISE

Praise and thank God for his limitless love for all
    his creation:
our desire to know him:
his equal love for those whom we find it
    hard to care for:

Pray for God's love to be in you and in all people,
    especially those
who wield political, religious and military power.

Lord, we are weak:
Uphold us.
Lord, we are narrow in mind and spirit:
Enlighten us.
Lord, we are cool in our affections:
Warm us.
Lord, we are insignificant:
But by your mercy we can be strong.

The first reading is from *Song at the Year's Turning*, by R. S. Thomas, published by Rupert Hart-Davis, 1955.

THE UNITED NATIONS ORGANISATION

*A reflection on the oneness of God's love
and the peace of the world*

We praise you, O God:
You are the Lord.
We acclaim you, O Lord:
You are the eternal Father.
We worship you, O Father:
And all creation worships you.
In you Lord is our hope:
Let us not be confounded at the last.

READING THE PREAMBLE TO THE CHARTER OF THE
UNITED NATIONS ORGANISATION

We, the Peoples of the United Nations, determined to
save succeeding generations from the scourge of war,
which twice in our lifetime has brought untold
sorrow to mankind,

and to reaffirm faith in fundamental human rights, in
the dignity and worth of the human person, in the
equal rights of men and women and of nations large
and small,

and to establish conditions under which justice and
respect for the obligations arising from treaties and
other sources of international law can be maintained,

and to promote social progress and better standards
of life in larger freedom,

and, for these ends,

to practise tolerance and live together in peace with
one another as good neighbours,

and to unite our strength to maintain international
peace and security, and to ensure, by the acceptance
of principles and the institution of methods, that
armed forces shall not be used, save in the common

interest, and to employ international machinery for
the promotion of the economic and social
advancement of all peoples,

have resolved to combine our efforts to accomplish these
aims.

READING MICAH 4:1-5. R.E.B.

In days to come
the mountain of the Lord's house
will be established higher than all other mountains,
towering above other hills.
Peoples will stream towards it;
many nations will go, saying,
'Let us go up to the mountain of the Lord,
to the house of Jacob's God,
that he may teach us his ways
and we may walk in his paths.'
For instruction issues from Zion,
the word of the Lord from Jerusalem.

He will judge between many peoples
and arbiter among great and distant nations.
They will hammer their swords into mattocks
and their spears into pruning-knives.
Nation will not take up sword against nation;
they will never again be trained for war.
Each man will sit under his own vine
or his own fig tree, with none to cause alarm.
The Lord of Hosts himself has spoken.
Other peoples may be loyal to their own deities,
but our loyalty will be for ever to the Lord our God.

PICTURE · PONDER · PRAY · PROMISE

Adore God, acclaim him Lord of justice, peace, and
human fellowship.

Pray for peace in the world
    between races, nations, factions and parties,
    fair distribution of the wealth of the earth,
    justice for oppressed minorities and political prisoners,
    between the Jewish People and the other nations.

A Prayer

    Lord of the future, the only ruler in eternity,
Set mankind free from the deadness of racial prejudice,
    nationalism and greed for power over others,
Enable the rich and powerful to find fulfilment in
    caring for the poor and weak;
Let the nations live together as one blood and
    fellowship,
    for you are brother to all mankind
    and by your blood we are set free from sin. Amen.

    Father of all:
    Make all one fellowship in you.
    Saviour of all:
    Save all mankind.
    Spirit in all:
    Inspire and perfect every nation.

The opening responses are adapted from the *Te Deum*, A.S.B. version.

MOTHER MARIA PILENKO

Good Friday 1945

When I survey the wondrous cross:
On which the Prince of Glory died;
My richest gain I count but loss:
And pour contempt on all my pride.

READING MARIA PILENKO: MARTYR

Elizabeth Pilenko came of a wealthy land-owning family in the south of Russia. She became a keen socialist revolutionary, and, during the years 1914-1917, her life was taken up with revolutionary activities. After the October Revolution she worked with extraordinary skill and daring in rescuing victims from the Terror. Later she became Mayor of her home town, working for justice between the Whites and the Reds, both of whom had resorted to violence against their opponents. She was denounced as a Bolshevist, tried and acquitted.

She found her way back to religious faith, and presented herself to the authorities of the Russian Church in Paris, announcing that she wished to become a religious, 'beginning at once, today,' and to found a monastery. She was not the traditional Russian Orthodox religious. 'I must go my way,' she said, 'I am for the suffering people.' In the early morning she was at the markets buying cheap food for the people she fed, bringing it back in a sack on her back. She was a familiar figure in the slum, in her poor black habit and her worn-out man's shoes.

When the German occupation took place, Mother Maria felt that her particular duty was to render all possible assistance to persecuted Jews. She knew that this would mean imprisonment and probably death. For a month the convent was a haven for Jews. Women and children were hidden. Money poured in to help them to escape. At the end of a month the Gestapo came. Mother

Maria was arrested and sent to the concentration camp at Ravensbruck.

She was known to the guards as 'that wonderful Russian nun', and it is doubtful whether they had any intention of killing her. She had been there two and a half years when a new block of buildings was erected in the camp, and the prisoners were told that these were to be hot baths. A day came when a few dozen prisoners from the women's quarters were lined up outside the buildings. One girl became hysterical. Mother Maria, who had not been selected, came up to her. 'Don't be frightened,' she said, 'Look, I shall take your turn,' and in line with the rest, she passed through the doors of the gas chamber. It was Good Friday, 1945.

READING PHILIPPIANS 2:5-11. R.E.B.

Take to heart among yourselves what you find in Christ Jesus:

'He was in the form of God;
yet he laid no claim to equality with God,
but made himself nothing, assuming the form of a slave.
Bearing the human likeness,
sharing the human lot,
he humbled himself,
and was obedient, even to the point of death,
death on a cross!
Therefore God raised him to the heights
and bestowed on him the name above all names,
that at the name of Jesus every knee should bow
– in heaven, on earth, and in the depths –
and every tongue acclaim,
"Jesus Christ is Lord"
to the glory of God the Father.'

PICTURE • PONDER • PRAY • PROMISE

A Prayer of Dedication

Lord Jesus, we see in you the perfect love of God:
**Hold us firm in this vision, always open
  to your call.**
Lord Jesus, you heal us by the offering of your life
  for us.
**Transfigure us with love, make us holy,
  make us perfect.**
Lord Jesus, as you gave yourself to save your world:
**May we give ourselves to you and to one another.
Amen.**

PASTOR PAUL SCHNEIDER

A Christian murdered by Nazis

The Lord is my shepherd:
Therefore can I lack nothing.
Though I walk through the valley of the shadow
of death:
I will fear no evil.
For you are with me:
Your rod and your staff comfort me.

READING JOHN 12:23-26. R.E.B.
THE ETERNAL WAY OF LIVING

Jesus said: 'The hour has come for the Son of Man to be glorified. In very truth I tell you, unless a grain of wheat falls into the ground and dies, it remains that and nothing more; but if it dies, it bears a rich harvest. Whoever loves himself is lost, but he who hates himself in this world will be kept safe for eternal life. If anyone is to serve me, he must follow me; where I am, there will my servant be. Whoever serves me will be honoured by the Father.'

READING THE MARTYRDOM OF PAUL SCHNEIDER

'Martyrdom is never the design of men; for the true martyr is he who has become the instrument of God, who has lost his will in the will of God, not lost it but found it, for he has found freedom in submission to God. The martyr no longer desires anything for himself, not even the glory of martyrdom.' Thus wrote T. S. Eliot in 'Murder in the Cathedral'.

Through faith man puts himself like a tool into the hand of God. It was thus that Paul Schneider, pastor at Dickenshied-Womrath, born August 29, 1897, near Kreuznach, Rhenish Prussia, became a chosen witness for the faith. When confronted by the antithesis of Christianity – the use of a lie as a political force – he called it by its name and therefore forfeited his life. He could not preach the Word without living it. And this he did in all simplicity, without hesitation, even when he found himself alone and at the mercy of his enemies. God had willed it so, and his instrument, his witness, obeyed. In this way, through a suffering not chosen but endured of his own free will, Paul Schneider was permitted to emulate his crucified Saviour.

It started in the very first year of the National Socialist regime, with a disciplinary transfer from his post. An ominous clash took place when Pastor Schneider, at the burial of a child of his parish, denounced the web of pagan mythology that for political reasons was being imposed upon the Christian concept of the hereafter. Now he had a foretaste of the ordeal that was to come. He was not among those who, resigning themselves to anticipated loss, possess as though they do not possess. He loved his wife and children with the unbroken strength of his great heart. No one can measure the abyss of suffering and renunciation through which he must have passed in order to be able to reply as he did to a friend warning him to be careful. 'Do you think,' he said, 'that God gave me children only that I might provide for their material welfare? Were they not entrusted to me in order that I might safeguard them for eternity?'

For Pastor Schneider, martyrdom came as a duty that he could not shirk. But in accepting the duty he made it a voluntary act, completely his own, willed and fought for with all his strength of soul.

He was arrested, then released under an order of expulsion. Despite the order he preached from the pulpit from which he had been banned and was arrested again. On July 24th, 1937, he was released from prison but at the same time expelled from the Rhineland. He ignored this order and stayed with his parish.

Pastor Schneider did not have long to wait for the final separation, which came on the day of the festival of thanksgiving for the harvest. The congregation was happy to see its pastor officiating as before. The decorated altar, the sermon, the joyful hymns of thanks – everything was as it had been in years gone by. Only a few intimates noticed that, after the blessing, the pastor surveyed his congregation with a look of mingled love and sorrow that gradually faded into detachment, as if the parting had already taken place.

There was still time to say the evening prayer at the bedside of his children.

Then they arrested him.

PICTURE • PONDER • PRAY • PROMISE

A PRAYER

> Father, we praise you for those who suffer
>   imprisonment,
>   ridicule and death in your service.
> Help us to serve you faithfully through Jesus Christ
>   your Son. Amen.

Pray for those who suffer persecution in any shape or form
>   for those whom hatred, fear or weakness have become
>   persecutors,
>   for all who work for freedom of thought and belief for
>   all mankind.

> Jesus said: 'He who loves his life:
> **Loses it.'**
> Jesus said: 'Whoever serves me:
> **Will be honoured by the Father.'**
> Let us go in confidence and peace of mind:
> **For God is love.**

The second reading is from *Dying we live*, ed Gollwitzer, Huhn and Scheider. Copyright Pantheon Press, New York. Reproduced by permission.

St Luke

The healing ministry of the church of Jesus

O Lord, open our lips:
To praise your healing name.
O Lord, heal us in truth:
And make us healers in your love.

READING LUKE 10:1-9. J.B.

The Lord appointed seventy-two and sent them out ahead of him, in pairs, to all the towns and places he himself was to visit.

He said to them, 'The harvest is rich but the labourers are few, so ask the Lord of the harvest to send labourers to his harvest. Start off now, but remember, I am sending you out like lambs among wolves. Carry no purse, no haversack, no sandals. Salute no one on the road. Whatever house you go into, let your first words be, "Peace to this house!" And if a man of peace lives there, your peace will go and rest on him; if not, it will come back to you. Stay in the same house, taking what food and drink they have to offer, for the labourer deserves his wages; do not move from house to house. Whenever you go into a town where they make you welcome, eat what is set before you. Cure those in it who are sick, and say, "The kingdom of God is very near to you."'

READING THE HEALING GOSPEL

The healing ministry of the church is an essential part of its whole ministry; without it, the gospel is not preached in its fulness, which perhaps explains part of the indifference of so many to the Church's message today.

The cause of much disease is to be found in wrong assumptions about God and about life, in wrong ways of thinking which create deep disharmony of the soul, in wrong attitudes to people and to the circumstances of life. In some cases there may be no short cut back to health and healing. The person who is sick must be taught to know God truly and to change his ways of thinking and to repent of his sins. Some will respond more quickly than others. But as soon as anyone begins with real faith to seek God, and to know him as the great reality, he will have set his feet on the road to health.

Faith is creative, and 'according to your faith so shall it be to you.' Faith is first a complete conviction that God is real, and that his life is within and that God is always good and loving and always working to heal and to perfect us in soul and body. Such faith must be so wholehearted and strong that, in the face of the most depressing circumstances, we can look up to God and know that all is well because we are in his hands and he cannot do else than work for our good. Faith of this kind is accompanied by intense love and confidence and by a ringing sense of joy that, when all other help seems to have failed, God is here and working and will work for our good. Such faith and love never fail to bring their reward.

So in faith we ask; knowing that our prayer will be answered.

PICTURE · PONDER · PRAY · PROMISE

A Prayer

> Thank you, O God, for the healing power
>   of the gospel of Jesus.
> Grant us a positive faith and a deep understanding
>   of your healing power,
> To take our share, to play our part, in the building of
>   your kingdom of wholeness and peace. Amen.

Thank God for St Luke, and for healers of every kind.

Pray for doctors, surgeons, nurses and all people in healing professions.

Pray for the healing of the nations and for peace on earth.

Praise God that he can surely bring healing and good out
of evil,
as surely as he raised Christ from the tomb.

Eternal God, Healing Lord:
Unite all minds in truth and love.
Eternal God, Healing Lord:
May your healing power flow through our lives.

The second reading is from *Healing Through the Power of Christ*,
by Jim Wilson, published by The Guild of Health. Reproduced by permission.

St Matthew

A reflection on St Matthew and conventional religion

Father, you are with us:
We are here to worship you.
Christ, you are with us:
In you is no darkness at all.
Spirit, you are with us:
In you we live and move and have our being.
Holy God, one and yet three:
We love you, because you first loved us.

Reading Matthew 9:9-13. J.B.
          Jesus, Matthew and Pharisees

Jesus saw a man named Matthew sitting by the customs house, and he said to him, 'Follow me.' He got up and followed him.

While Jesus was at dinner in the house it happened that a number of tax collectors and sinners came to sit at the table with Jesus and his disciples. When the Pharisees saw this, they said to his disciples, 'Why does your master eat with tax collectors and sinners?' When he heard this he replied, 'It is not the healthy who need the doctor, but the sick. Go and learn the meaning of the words: What I want is mercy, not sacrifice. And indeed I did not come to call the virtuous, but sinners.'

Reading A Prayer by Malcolm Boyd

God:
Take fire and burn our guilt and our lying hypocrisies.
Take water and wash our brother's blood which we have
    caused to be shed.
Take hot sunlight and dry the tears of those we have hurt,
    and heal their wounded souls, minds and bodies.
Take love and root it in our hearts, so that brotherhood
    may grow, transforming the dry desert of our
    prejudices and hatreds.

Take our imperfect prayers and purify them, so that we
   mean what we pray and are prepared to give ourselves
   to you along with our words;
Through Jesus Christ, who did not disdain to take our
   humanness upon him and live among us, sharing our
   life, our joys, and our pains.

PICTURE • PONDER • PRAY • PROMISE

Thank God for his mercy and forgiveness.

Praise him that you are forgiven.
Pray for true repentance
   for objectivity about yourself
   for an open heart to God's love for you.

> Lord:
> **Take us**
> Lord:
> **Break us**
> Lord:
> **Make of us what you will. Amen.**

The second reading is from *Are You Running With Me, Jesus?* by Malcolm Boyd,
1967, Heinemann Publishers (Oxford) Ltd. Reproduced by permission.

ALL SAINTS

*A thanksgiving to God for all his saints
and for our own call to sainthood*

O Lord, open our lips:
To praise you for all your saints.
We praise you for holy lives:
Of every generation.
They lived in your power and strength:
They died in the peace of your love.

READING   THE SAINTS IN HEAVEN

Bright, bright
The fellowship of saints in light,
Far, far beyond all earthly sight.
No plague can blight, no foe destroy
United here they live in love:
O then, above how deep their joy!

Set free
By Jesu's mortal wounds are we,
Blest with rich gifts – and more shall be.
Blessings has he in endless store:
Some drops are showered upon us here;
What when we hear the ocean's roar?

Deep, deep
The feast of life and peace they keep
In that fair world beyond death's sleep.
Our hearts will leap their joys to see
Who, with the Lamb's dear mercy graced,
All sorrows past, reign glad and free.

READING MATTHEW 5:1-10. R.E.B.
          SAINTLINESS ON EARTH

When he saw the crowds, Jesus went up a mountain.
There he sat down, and when his disciples had gathered

round him, he began to address them. And this is the teaching he gave:

Blessed are the poor in spirit;
    the Kingdom of Heaven is theirs.
Blessed are the sorrowful;
    they shall find consolation.
Blessed are the gentle;
    they shall have the earth for their possession.
Blessed are those who hunger and thirst to see right
        prevail;
    they shall be satisfied.
Blessed are those who show mercy;
    mercy shall be shown to them.
Blessed are those whose hearts are pure;
    they shall see God.
Blessed are the peacemakers;
    they shall be called God's children.
Blessed are those who are persecuted in the cause of right;
    the Kingdom of Heaven is theirs.

PICTURE · PONDER · PRAY · PROMISE

A PRAYER

O Father of creation, greater in glory than we can describe,
    more full of love than we can imagine,
As you enabled your saints of old
So make us able now,
To reach that holiness of life and love which we can
    never reach,
Save by the grace of your Spirit,
And the perfect sacrifice of Jesus on the cross of Calvary.
Amen.

Praise God that he makes possible the holiness that our
best efforts can never attain.
Praise him for saints on earth known to you.
Pray for the strength to be holy as he is holy.
Pray for grace to overcome those difficulties and sins
that face you today.

Holy Jesus:
Make us holy.
Holy Spirit:
Make us strong.
Holy Father:
Make us aware of your life and love:
in all we do and say.

The first reading is from *Threshold of Light*, ed. by A. M. Allchin & E. de Waal, published by Darton Longman and Todd. Verse 1 by Robert Jones, Caergybi (1731-1806). Verses 2 and 3 – anonymous. Trans H.A.H.

MARTIN LUTHER KING

The price of a Christian victory

THE KILLING OF DR KING

The Reverend Dr Martin Luther King was leader of the 'Southern Christian Leadership Conference' in the USA. He dedicated his life to non-violent struggle for racial equality and brotherhood. He won the Nobel Peace Prize. In April, 1968, he went to Memphis, Tennessee, to assist a strike that demanded equal pay and conditions for negro and white municipal workers. He knew of threats to his life, but urged his supporters to press on to the 'promised land' of equality and racial harmony, a land which he believed he had seen from the mountaintop of faith. The next day, he was killed.

O Lord, open our lips:
And open our eyes to your love.
O Lord, open our hearts:
To live for your justice and truth.

READING DEUTERONOMY 34. T.E.V.
THE DEATH OF MOSES

Moses went up from the plains of Moab to Mount Nebo, to the top of Mount Pisgah east of Jericho, and there the Lord showed him the whole land: the territory of Gilead as far north as the town of Dan; the entire territory of Naphtali; the territories of Ephraim and Manasseh; the territory of Judah as far west as the Mediterranean Sea; the southern part of Judah; and the plain that reaches from Zoar to Jericho, the city of palm-trees. Then the Lord said to Moses, This is the land that I promised Abraham, Isaac and Jacob I would give to their descendants. I have let you see it, but I will not let you go there.

So Moses, the Lord's servant, died there in the land of Moab, as the Lord had said he would. The Lord buried him in a valley in Moab, opposite the town of Bethpeor, but to this day no one knows the exact place of his burial. Moses was a hundred and twenty years old when he died; he was as strong as ever, and his eyesight was still good. The people of Israel mourned for him for thirty days in the plains of Moab.

Joshua son of Nun was filled with wisdom, because Moses had appointed him to be his successor. The people of Israel obeyed Joshua and kept the commands that the Lord had given them through Moses.

There has never been a prophet in Israel like Moses; the Lord spoke with him face to face. No other prophet has ever done miracles and wonders like those that the Lord sent Moses to perform against the king of Egypt, his officials and the entire country. No other prophet has been able to do the great and terrifying things that Moses did in the sight of all Israel.

READING PART OF DR KING'S SPEECH AT THE MARCH ON WASHINGTON FOR JOBS AND FREEDOM, 1963

As Martin Luther King, jr., began to speak, the hush to a silence of a cathedral fell over the crowd. Like a well-tuned church bell, his voice pealed the marchers' message across the huge mall between the Lincoln Memorial and the Washington Monument.

'I have a dream,' he cried.

The crowd roared. 'Tell us!'

'I have a dream – that the sons of former slaves and the sons of former slave owners will be able to sit together at the table of brotherhood.'

'Yes! Yes! I see it!' roared the crowds.

'I have a dream that my four little children will one day live in a nation where they will not be judged by the colour of their skin, but by the content of their character.'

'Oh, yes! Dream on! Dream!' cried the crowd.

PICTURE • PONDER • PRAY • PROMISE

A PRAYER

Martin Luther King once said 'Our aim must never be to defeat or humiliate the white man, but to win his friendship and understanding':

O God, Father of mankind, you are neither black, nor brown, nor yellow, nor white. Yet, Father, we know that you are Love. Help us to love and gain enrichment from the glorious variety of peoples who live on your earth. Amen.

Pray for racial harmony, especially where prejudice
    is worst.

Pray for an understanding and a love for those of
    other faiths, philosophies and traditions.

Pray for peace in God's world, especially where hate
    is most fierce.

Pray for the Jewish people and all who follow the law
    of Moses.

> Lord, use us today:
> **To continue your work of reconciliation.**
> Lord, use us today:
> **To sow seeds of harmony between people we meet.**
> Lord, live through us today:
> **For Jesus's sake. Amen.**

The extract from Martin Luther King's speech in Washington is from *Marching to Freedom*, ed by Robert M. Bleiweiss, published by Penguin, USA, 1969.

St Francis of Assisi

*A reflection on the romance and poetry
and the humility and discipline of Francis*

O Lord, open our lips:
And our mouths shall proclaim your praise.
Righteous are you, our Father God:
May our lives reflect your goodness.

READING LUKE 9:57-62. J.B.
THE ABSOLUTE DEMANDS OF JESUS

As they travelled along they met a man on the road who said to Jesus, 'I will follow you wherever you go.' Jesus answered, 'Foxes have holes and the birds of the air have nests, but the Son of Man has nowhere to lay his head.'

Another to whom Jesus said, 'Follow me,' replied, 'Let me go and bury my father first.' But he answered, 'Leave the dead to bury their dead; your duty is to go and spread the news of the kingdom of God.'

Another said, 'I will follow you, sir, but first let me go and say good-bye to my people at home.' Jesus said to him, 'Once the hand is laid on the plough, no one who looks back is fit for the kingdom of heaven.'

READING ST FRANCIS SPEAKS OF THE ORDER HE FOUNDED

'Foxes have holes, and birds of the air have nests: but the Son of man has nowhere to lay his head.'

Francis and his first brethren wished to be no richer than Our Lord in his poverty. They therefore never entered any of the houses in the town, except as Christ's messengers of peace or as beggars. Instead they sought caves or shacks in the fields outside the city, and there, hidden from men's gaze, they devoted themselves to prayer and penance.

Many people were touched by God's grace when they met the brethren, but there were few of these who had the courage to throw in their lot with them. Francis said to

Brother Giles: 'Our Order is like a trawler, who throws his net into the sea and gathers an enormous number of fish; the little ones he throws back into the water, but the big ones he keeps.' How true this was, as was shown later, when men and women with big and generous hearts were received into the Order, while those with small minds and faint hearts were rejected.

PICTURE · PONDER · PRAY · PROMISE

PRAYER

St Francis is said to have given away a book of the
Gospels to feed a starving old woman:
**Teach us to live in the Gospel spirit
and not to cling to the letter, O Lord.**

St Francis is celebrated for his love of the natural order,
especially wild animals:
Teach us to love and care for the earth, O Lord.

St Francis renewed the church's mission
by his example:
Teach us to share our faith, O Lord.

St Francis spoke to the powerful and influenced
the rulers of church and state:
**Teach us to care for human society
and all its children.**

The Lord says: 'Whom shall I send, who will go
for us?'
'Lord, here am I, send me.'

The second reading is from *St. Francis of Assisi* by Walter Hauser, published by Thomas & Hudson.

ST PETER: COWARD AND ROCK

A life transformed by failure and forgiveness

O Lord, open our lips:
To praise and adore you.
In Jesus you show us yourself:
The Christ, Son of God, our Saviour.

READING MATTHEW 16:13-19. R.S.V.
PETER – A MOMENT OF GLORY

When Jesus came into the district of Caesarea Philippi, he asked his disciples, 'Who do men say that the Son of Man is?' And they said, 'Some say John the Baptist, others, say Elijah, and others Jeremiah or one of the prophets.' He said to them, 'But who do you say that I am?' Simon Peter replied, 'You are the Christ, the Son of the living God.' And Jesus answered him, 'Blessed are you, Simon Bar-Jona! For flesh and blood has not revealed this to you, but my Father who is in heaven. And I tell you, you are Peter, and on this rock I will build my church, and the powers of death shall not prevail against it. I will give you the keys of the kingdom of heaven, and whatever you bind on earth shall be bound in heaven, and whatever you loose on earth shall be loosed in heaven.

READING MATTHEW 26:69-75. R.S.V.
PETER – A MOMENT OF BITTER FAILURE

Now Peter was sitting outside in the courtyard. And a maid came up to him, and said, 'You also were with Jesus the Galilean.' But he denied it before them all, saying, 'I do not know what you mean.' And when he went out to the porch, another maid saw him, and she said to the bystanders, 'This man was with Jesus of Nazareth.' And again he denied it with an oath, 'I do not know the man.' After a little while the bystanders came up and said to Peter, 'Certainly you are also one of them, for your accent betrays you.' Then he began to invoke a curse on himself and to swear, 'I do not know the man.' And immediately the cock crowed. And Peter remembered the saying of Jesus, 'Before the cock crows, you will deny me three times.' And he went out and wept bitterly.

READING PETER – A POET'S COMMENT

My son,
Will you not let God manage his own business?
He was a carpenter, and knows his trade
Better perhaps, than we did, having had
Some centuries of experience; nor will He,
Like a bad workman, blame the tools wherewith
He builds His City of Zion here on earth.
For God founded His Church, not upon John,
The loved disciple, that lay so close to His heart
And knew His mind – not upon John, but Peter;
Peter the liar, Peter the coward, Peter
The rock, the common man. John was all gold,
And gold is rare; the work might wait while God
Ransacked the corners of the earth to find
Anther John; Peter is the stone
Whereof the world is made.

PICTURE · PONDER · PRAY · PROMISE

A PRAYER

Lord, you have shown us the power of your mercy and
    forgiveness in the life of Peter:
Mend our lives,
Make good our foolishness,
Take the debris of our failings
And make us strong in your service. Amen.

Pray for true repentance:
Pray for the grace to accept God's forgiveness and be set
  free from guilt and shame.
Praise God that as he brought resurrection life from the
  misery of Calvary, so he can turn our mistakes and sins
  into good and holy living.

Pray for those who find it hard to forgive themselves.
  for those who dare not trust the mercy of God.

> Father, Lord of the universe:
> **Make us revere your greatness.**
> Jesus, Prince of peace:
> **Make us holy in every way.**
> Spirit, giver of resurrection life:
> **Keep us healthy in soul and body.**
> God, whose faithfulness never fails:
> **Transform us to do your will.**

The third reading is from *The Zeal of Thine House*, by Dorothy L. Sayers
published by Gollancz. Reproduced by permission of David Higham
Associates.

St Lawrence:
A Sense of Values

*A reflection on true wealth
and divine love*

INTRODUCTION

St. Lawrence was martyred in 258 A.D., burned to death on an iron grid. He had enraged the persecuting authorities of Rome by failing to hand over the church's Gospel Books, cash and valuables. Instead he assembled the poor, sick and lame people whom the Christians were feeding and caring for. These people, he said, were the church's true treasure.

O God, maker of the worlds:
We adore you, source of true riches.
O God, saviour of mankind:
You are our true hope and glory.

READING MATTHEW 6:19-24. T.E.V.
GOD AND POSSESSIONS

Do not store up riches for yourself here on earth, where moths and rust destroy, and robbers break in and steal. Instead, store up riches for yourselves in heaven, where moths and rust cannot destroy, and robbers cannot break in and steal. For your heart will always be where your riches are.

The eyes are like a lamp for the body. If your eyes are sound, your whole body will be full of light; but if your eyes are no good, your body will be in darkness. So if the light in you is darkness, how terribly dark it will be!

No one can be the slave of two masters; he will hate one and love the other; he will be loyal to one and despise the other. You cannot serve both God and money.

READING 'THINGS': A MEDITATION

I remember a story, Lord, from the early days of the Church,
    during the Decian persecution in Rome.
The authorities burst into the church to loot its treasures.
Laurentius, a deacon, pointed to widows and orphans
    being cared for, the sick being nursed, the poor having
        their needs supplied.
These are the treasures of the church.

    Things are good in themselves, Lord.
    They are part of creation.
    How would we live without them?
    The ambulance that drives the sick to hospital.
    The bus that takes the men to work.
    The pan that cooks our food.
    The clothes that keep us warm.
    The books that help us learn.

    Things have beauty too, Lord.
    Life would be less without enjoyment of it.
    The shimmering beauty of finely cut glass.
    The aesthetic design of a piece of furniture.
    The elegant cut of a dress.
    The consummate skill of a sculpture.
    The melody of a musical instrument.

    The eye that is unsound sees only part of the truth.
    It looks through a filter as opaque as a cataract.
    It looks at life and distorts what it sees.
    It sees a welter of things and is eager to make them
        possessions.
    It competes with the hoarding church – those silver
        and jewelled sets of sacrament vessels, never used,
        never seen, never removed from their dusty corner in
        some ecclesiastical safe.

Enable me, Lord, to enjoy the usefulness and beauty of
    things;
Prevent me investing in them my all, hoarding them and
    turning them into my idol, my god.

Lead me to invest my all in the treasures of Laurentius.
Lead me to use things in your service, and not in my own.

PICTURE · PONDER · PRAY · PROMISE

Thank God for your possessions, especially those dearest
to you.
Pray for a sense of values that will set you free from greed.

Thank God for the earth and its riches.
Pray for those who have great wealth.
Pray for government and industries with power over life
on our planet.

A PRAYER

O God, who gave to your servant Lawrence
grace to be a wise guardian of the church's treasures,
a faithful attender to his duty,
a bold witness to the faith;
Stir us to an equal devotion, and prepare us for the
judgement when all secrets shall be disclosed.
Amen.

Lay not up treasures upon earth:
We cannot serve God and money.
God, our true fulfilment upon earth:
All that we have is yours.

The second reading is from *A Kind of Praying*, by Rex Chapman, 1970, SCM
Press. Reproduced by permission.

St Barnabas:
Son of Encouragement

*A reflection on a saint of great faith
and sensivity to other people*

Introduction

Overshadowed by Paul and less famous than Mark, Barnabas was nevertheless the vital link in their development as Christians. He is the true and faithful minister, whose less public and remarkable talents lie beneath the work of others.

> We praise your name, O Lord:
> **For saints in every age.**
> We thank you for their lives:
> **And pray for grace to follow in their way.**

Readings St Barnabas in The Acts of the Apostles T.E.V.

Acts 4:32-37
Barnabas among the earliest Christians

The group of believers was one in mind and heart. No one said that any of his belongings was his own, but they all shared with one another everything they had. With great power the apostles gave witness to the resurrection of the Lord Jesus, and God poured rich blessings on them all. There was no one in the group who was in need. Those who owned fields or houses would sell them, bring the money received from the sale, and hand it over to the apostles; and the money was distributed to each one according to his need.

And so it was that Joseph, a Levite born in Cyprus, whom the apostles called Barnabas (which means 'One Who Encourages'), sold a field he owned, brought the money, and handed it over to the apostles.

ACTS 9:26-28 BARNABAS THE RECONCILER

Saul went to Jerusalem and tried to join the disciples. But they would not believe that he was a disciple, and they were all afraid of him. Then Barnabas came to his help and took him to the apostles. He explained to them how Saul had seen the Lord on the road and that the Lord had spoken to him. He also told them how boldly Saul had preached in the name of Jesus in Damascus. And so Saul stayed with them and went all over Jerusalem, preaching boldly in the name of the Lord.

ACTS 11:19-26 BARNABAS THE PASTOR

Some of the believers who were scattered by the persecution which took place when Stephen was killed went as far as Phoenicia, Cyprus and Antioch, telling the message to Jews only. But other believers, men from Cyprus and Cyrene, went to Antioch and proclaimed the message to Gentiles also, telling them the Good News about the Lord Jesus. The Lord's power was with them, and a great number of people believed and turned to the Lord.

The news about this reached the church in Jerusalem, so they sent Barnabas to Antioch. When he arrived and saw how God had blessed the people, he was glad and urged them all to be faithful and true to the Lord with all their hearts. Barnabas was a good man, full of the Holy Spirit and faith, and many people were brought to the Lord.

Then Barnabas went to Tarsus to look for Saul. When he found him, he took him to Antioch, and for a whole year the two met with the people of the church and taught a large group. It was at Antioch that the believers were first called Christians.

ACTS 13:1-12 BARNABAS TRAVELS WITH PAUL

In the church at Antioch there were some prophets and teachers: Barnabas, Simeon (called the Black), Lucius (from Cyrene), Manaen (who had been brought up with Herod the governor), and Saul. While they were serving the Lord and fasting, the Holy Spirit said to them, 'Set apart for me Barnabas and Saul, to do the work to which I have called them.'

They fasted and prayed, placed their hands on them, and sent them off.

Having been sent by the Holy Spirit, Barnabas and Saul went to Seleucia and sailed from there to the island of Cyprus. When they arrived at Salamis, they preached the word of God in the synagogues. They had John Mark with them to help in the work.

They went all the way across the island to Paphos, where they met a certain magician named Bar-Jesus, a Jew who claimed to be a prophet. He was a friend of the governor of the island, Sergius Paulus, who was an intelligent man. The governor called Barnabas and Saul before him because he wanted to hear the word of God. But they were opposed by the magician Elymas (that is his name in Greek), who tried to turn the governor away from the faith. Then Saul – also known as Paul – was filled with the Holy Spirit; he looked straight at the magician and said, 'You son of the Devil! You are the enemy of everything that is good. You are full of all kinds of evil tricks, and you always keep trying to turn the Lord's truths into lies! The Lord's hand will come down on you now; you will be blind and will not see the light of day for a time.'

At once Elymas felt a dark mist cover his eyes, and he walked about trying to find someone to lead him by the hand. When the governor saw what had happened, he believed; for he was greatly amazed at the teaching about the Lord.

ACTS 15:36-40 BARNABAS, IN CONFLICT, CHOSE THE PATH OF FORGIVENESS:
Some time later Paul said to Barnabas, 'Let us go back and visit our brothers in every town where we preached the word of the Lord, and let us find out how they are getting on.' Barnabas wanted to take John Mark with them, but Paul did not think it was right to take him, because he had not stayed with them to the end of their mission, but had turned back and left them in Pamphylia. There was a sharp argument, and they separated: Barnabas took Mark

and sailed off for Cyprus, while Paul chose Silas and left, commended by the believers to the care of the Lord's grace. He went through Syria and Cilicia, strengthening the churches.

PICTURE • PONDER • PRAY • PROMISE

A PRAYER

> Lord, you endowed St Barnabas with great pastoral gifts.
> Help us to care as he cared and to understand others with compassion. Amen.

Praise God for Barnabas and his gift of encouraging others.

Thank God that Barnabas saw the true worth of John Mark.

Pray for all Christians, that they will be filled with discernment and love.

Pray for discernment and love in yourself.

> Give us this day, O Father of Creation,
>   true reverence:
> **To realise your presence.**
> Give us humility:
> **To know our own needs,**
> Give us trust:
> **To ask your help.**
> Give us obedience:
> **To do your will.**

157

St Andrew: Sharing the Gospel

St Andrew was the first missionary for Jesus.
He introduced Peter to the Lord. He is the
scarcely known man whose influence lasts for ever.

O Lord, open our lips:
To tell of your love and your truth.
Make us faithful in your service:
Use us to your glory.

READING JOHN 1:35-42. T.E.V.
ANDREW BRINGS PETER TO JESUS

The next day John was standing there again with two of his disciples, when he saw Jesus walking by. 'There is the Lamb of God!' he said.

The two disciples heard him say this and went with Jesus. Jesus turned, saw them following him, and asked, 'What are you looking for?' They answered, 'Where do you live, Rabbi?' (This word means 'Teacher').

'Come and see,' he answered. (It was then about four o'clock in the afternoon). So they went with him and saw where he lived, and spent the rest of that day with him.

One of them was Andrew, Simon Peter's brother. At once he found his brother Simon and told him, 'We have found the Messiah.' (This word means 'Christ'). Then he took Simon to Jesus.

Jesus looked at him and said, 'Your name is Simon son of John, but you will be called Cephas.' (This is the same as Peter and means 'a rock').

READING WE ARE ALL WITNESSES

It was through lay men and women much more than through the ordained clergy whether missionaries.or Africans, that the church grew. The coast trader thrusting up country into new villages, or the junior government officer transferred to clerkship in the District Commissioner's office or as a dresser in the hospital: such a man gathered others round him on Sunday morning for worship; and the church grew. Ask for the story of the beginning of the church in a village or small town anywhere in Africa, and the chances are you will be told, not how missionary X or African Pastor Y came and preached in the village street but how trader A – a man or woman from a strange town – or schoolboy B, who went from the village to seek schooling and came back a church member, asked the chief to allot a piece of land for the erection of a bamboo or mud chapel, and with the aid of a few men erected it.

PICTURE · PONDER · PRAY · PROMISE

Thank God for Andrew and for many thousands like him
    for those who have introduced us to Jesus and his
        Way of Life
    for opportunities to be 'Andrew' for others.

A PRAYER

    We are grateful, Lord, for Andrew and the simple way
    he shared his faith. May we, with equal sensitivity,
    make your truth clear in word and action. Amen.

    Lord, let us go in peace:
    To do your work this day.
    Lord, let us go in peace:
    To share your love with all people.

The second reading is from *Christianity and the new Africa*, by T. A. Beetham, published by Pall Mall Press Ltd.

St Matthias: An Unknown

A reflection and thanksgiving for the man who replaced Judas Iscariot, the betrayer of Jesus. Judas is far more famous, but Matthias and millions like him have continued the work of Jesus, and brought true life to millions more.

We praise you, O God:
For your steadfast love.
We praise you, O God:
For your sacrifice on the cross.
We praise you, O God:
For the conquest of death.
We praise you, O God:
Eternally King.

READING ACTS 1:15-26. R.E.B.
THE CHOOSING OF MATTHIAS

Peter stood up before the assembled brotherhood, about one hundred and twenty in all, and said: 'My friends, the prophecy in scripture, which the Holy Spirit uttered concerning Judas through the mouth of David, was bound to come true; Judas acted as guide to those who arrested Jesus – he was one of our number and had his place in this ministry. (After buying a plot of land with the price of his villainy, this man fell headlong and burst open so that all his entrails spilled out; everyone in Jerusalem came to hear of this, and in their own language they named the plot Akeldama, which means 'Blood Acre'.) 'The words I have in mind', Peter continued, 'are in the book of Psalms: "Let this homestead fall desolate; let there be none to inhabit it." And again, "Let his charge be given to another." Therefore one of those who bore us company all the while the Lord Jesus was going about among us, from his baptism by John until the day when he was taken up from us – one of those must now join us as a witness to his resurrection.'

Two names were put forward: Joseph, who was known as Barsabbas and bore the added name of Justus, and Matthias. Then they prayed and said, 'You know the hearts of everyone, Lord; declare which of these two you have chosen to receive this office of ministry and apostleship which Judas abandoned to go where he belonged.' They drew lots, and the lot fell to Matthias; so he was elected to be an apostle with the other eleven.

READING A HISTORIAN COMMENTS ON CHRISTIAN LIVING

I have nothing to say at the finish except that if one wants a permanent rock in life and goes deep enough for it, it is difficult for historical events to shake it. There are times when we can never meet the future with sufficient elasticity of mind, especially if we are locked in the contemporary systems of thought. We can do worse than remember a principle which both gives us a firm rock and leaves us maximum elasticity of our minds: the principle:
Hold to Christ, and for the rest be totally uncommitted.

PICTURE • PONDER • PRAY • PROMISE

A PRAYER

Lord God, Father of Creation,
We praise you for all the unknown Christians who have
    lived before us:
Help us to be faithful,
May we play our part in building your Kingdom
    of love. Amen.

Praise God for those who serve him faithfully
    for those who serve and care for us.
    for those who have given up success for the call of duty.

Pray for the unknown saints of the world,
    and for those who are greedy for fame and wealth.

O Lord:
To whom all people matter.
O Lord:
Who sees true worth and holiness.
O Lord:
Infinite in love and care.
We praise your holy name:
For you, O Lord, know all mankind by name.

The second reading is from *Christianity and History*, by Herbert Butterfield, George Bell & Sons Ltd, an imprint of HarperCollins Publishers Ltd. Reproduced by permission.

MARY OF NAZARETH

A thanksgiving for Mary, mother of Jesus

O Lord, open our lips:
And our mouth shall proclaim your praise.
We praise you for Mary of Nazareth:
Mother of Christ, our Lord and our God.

READING LUKE 1:26-38. T.E.V.
THE STORY OF THE ANNUNCIATION

In the sixth month of Elizabeth's pregnancy God sent the Angel Gabriel to a town in Galilee named Nazareth. He had a message for a girl promised in marriage to a man named Joseph, who was a descendant of King David. The girl's name was Mary. The angel came to her and said, 'Peace be with you! The Lord is with you and has greatly blessed you!'

Mary was deeply troubled by the angel's message, and she wondered what his words meant. The angel said to her, 'Don't be afraid, Mary; God has been gracious to you. You will become pregnant and give birth to a son, and you will name him Jesus. He will be great and will be called the Son of the Most High God. The Lord God will make him a king, as his ancestor David was, and he will be the king of the descendants of Jacob for ever; his kingdom will never end!'

Mary said to the angel, 'I am a virgin. How, then, can this be?' The angel answered, 'The Holy Spirit will come on you, and God's power will rest upon you. For this reason the holy child will be called the Son of God. Remember your relative Elizabeth. It is said that she cannot have children, but she herself is now six months pregnant, even though she is very old. For there is nothing that God cannot do.'

'I am the Lord's servant,' said Mary; 'may it happen to me as you have said.' And the angel left her.

READING THE ANNUNCIATION

Nothing will ease the pain to come
Though now she sits in ecstasy
And let it have its way with her.
The angel's shadow in the room
Is lightly lifted as if he
Had never terrified her there.

The furniture again returns
To its old simple state. She can
Take comfort from the things she knows
Though in her heart new loving burns,
Something she never gave to man
or god before, and this god grows

Most like a man. She wonders how
To pray at all, what thanks to give
And whom to give them to. 'Alone
To all men's eyes I now must go,'
She thinks, 'And by myself must live
With a strange child that is my own.'

So from her ecstasy she moves
And turns to human things at last
(Announcing angels set aside).
It is a human child she loves
Though a god stirs beneath her breast
And great salvations grip her side.

PICTURE • PONDER • PRAY • PROMISE

Praise God for Mary, her faith, her readiness,
    her gentleness
   for Mary's faithfulness in caring for Jesus as he grew up,
   for Mary's watching by the cross and her devotion to
     Jesus, even as he died.

Pray for mothers and their nurture of children
for mothers who see their children in sickness
and trouble,
for your own mother.

Pray for families in every part of the world
for a true valuing of family life by governments and
those who have power over families.

Pray that the family life of Mary and Joseph will guide
all families.

A PRAYER

We beseech you, O Lord,
to pour your grace into our hearts;
that as we have known the incarnation
of your Son Jesus Christ
by the message of an angel,
so by his cross and passion
we may be brought to the glory of his resurrection;
through Jesus Christ our Lord. Amen.

By the prayers of Mary and all of God's saints
Lord, make us worthy of the Promise of Christ

The second reading is from *A Sense of the World*, by Elizabeth Jennings,
Carcanet 1958.

THE CONVERSION OF ST PAUL

*A thanksgiving for St Paul, his dramatic conversion
and his vision of Christ in all Christ's people*

O Lord, source of all light and truth:
We praise your glory.
O Lord, healer of blindness of spirit:
We adore your truth.
O Lord, teacher of love and life:
We await your guiding Spirit.

READING ACTS 9:1-19 T.E.V. PAUL ENCOUNTERS JESUS:
'I AM JESUS WHOM YOU PERSECUTE'

In the meantime Saul kept up his violent threats of
murder against the followers of the Lord. He went to the
High Priest and asked for letters of introduction to the
synagogues in Damascus, so that if he should find there
any followers of the Way of the Lord, he would be able to
arrest them, both men and women, and bring them back
to Jerusalem.

As Saul was coming near the city of Damascus,
suddenly a light from the sky flashed round him. He fell
to the ground and heard a voice saying to him, 'Saul, Saul!
Why do you persecute me?'

'Who are you, Lord?' he asked.

'I am Jesus, whom you persecute,' the voice said. 'But
get up and go into the city, where you will be told what
you must do.'

The men who were travelling with Saul had stopped,
not saying a word; they heard the voice but could not see
anyone. Saul got up from the ground and opened his eyes,
but could not see a thing. So they took him by the hand
and led him into Damascus. For three days he was not
able to see, and during that time he did not eat or drink
anything.

There was a Christian in Damascus named Ananias.
He had a vision, in which the Lord said to him, 'Ananias!'

'Here I am, Lord,' he answered.

The Lord said to him, 'Get ready and go to Straight Street, and at the house of Judas ask for a man from Tarsus named Saul. He is praying and in a vision he has seen a man named Ananias come in and place his hands on him so that he might see again.'

Ananias answered, 'Lord, many people have told me about this man and about all the terrible things he has done to your people in Jerusalem. And he has come to Damascus with authority from the chief priests to arrest all who worship you.'

The Lord said to him, 'Go, because I have chosen him to serve me, to make my name known to Gentiles and kings and to the people of Israel. And I myself will show him all that he must suffer for my sake.'

So Ananias went, entered the house where Saul was, and placed his hands on him. 'Brother Saul,' he said, 'the Lord has sent me – Jesus himself, who appeared to you on the road as you were coming here. He sent me so that you might see again and be filled with the Holy Spirit.' At once something like fish scales fell from Saul's eyes, and he was able to see again. He stood up and was baptised; and after he had eaten, his strength came back.

READING A TWENTIETH CENTURY VISION OF CHRIST

I was in an underground train, a crowded train in which all sorts of people jostled together, sitting and strap-hanging – workers of every description going home at the end of the day. Quite suddenly I saw with my mind, but as vividly as a wonderful picture, Christ in them all. But I saw more than that; not only Christ in every one of them, living in them, dying in them, rejoicing in them, sorrowing in them – but because He was in them, and because they were here, the whole world was here too, here in this underground train not only the world as it was at that moment, not only all the people in all the countries of the world, but all those people who had lived in the past, and all those yet to come.

I came out into the street and walked for a long time in the crowds. It was the same here, on every side, in every passer-by, everywhere – Christ . . .

I saw, too, the reverence that everyone must have for a sinner; instead of condoning his sin, which is in reality his utmost sorrow, one must comfort Christ who is suffering in him. And this reverence must be paid even to those sinners whose souls seem to be dead, because it is Christ, who is the life of the soul, who is dead in them: they are His tombs, and Christ in the tomb is potentially the risen Christ. For the same reason, no one of us who has fallen into mortal sin himself must ever lose hope . . .

After a few days the 'vision' faded. People looked the same again, there was no longer the same shock of insight for me each time I was face to face with another human being. Christ was hidden again; indeed, through the years to come I would have to seek for Him, and usually I could find Him in others – and still more in myself – only through a deliberate and blind act of faith. But if the 'vision' had faded, the knowledge had not; on the contrary, that knowledge, touched by a ray of the Holy Spirit, is like a tree touched by the sun – it puts out leaf and flowers, bearing fruit and blossom from splendour to splendour.

PICTURE · PONDER · PRAY · PROMISE

A PRAYER

Lord, we thank you that you can show us yourself
    today,
    as you encountered Paul on the Damascus road.
Set us free from the blindness of selfishness and sin,
    make us see life with your eyes. Amen.

Praise God that Jesus interprets life for those who wish
    to understand.
Pray to have his vision of the world
    to see as he sees, to act as he acts.

Pray for those who feel no need of God, or love for
    other people
    for those who have rejected the gospel of Jesus.

    Christ is like a single body:
    Which has many parts.
    All of us are Christ's body:
    Each one a part of him.
    God is love:
    Christ's love is in our hearts.

The second reading is from *A Rocking Horse Catholic* by Caryll Houselander, Sheed & Ward Ltd. Reproduced by permission.

From Law and Guilt to Love and Grace

*A reflection of how God worked in the life
of one twentieth century Christian*

O God our Father:
Your grace is our deepest need.
Open the fears that seal our hearts and minds:
Let our lives proclaim your praise!

Reading Galatians 2:16-21. T.E.V.
God's saving gift of faith

Yet we know that a person is put right with God only through faith in Jesus Christ, never by doing what the Law requires. We, too, have believed in Christ Jesus in order to be put right with God through our faith in Christ, and not by doing what the Law requires. For no one is put right with God by doing what the Law requires. If, then, as we try to be put right with God by our union with Christ, we are found to be sinners as much as the Gentiles are – does this mean that Christ is serving the cause of sin? By no means! If I start to rebuild the system of the Law that I tore down, then I show myself to be someone who breaks the Law. So far as the Law is concerned, however, I am dead – killed by the Law itself – in order that I might live for God. I have been put to death with Christ on his cross, so that it is no longer I who live, but it is Christ who lives in me. This life that I live now, I live by faith in the Son of God, who loved me and gave his life for me. I refuse to reject the grace of God. But if a person is put right with God through the Law, it means that Christ died for nothing!

Reading A life transformed

I first met him in 1945. He had come straight from the Army to university, and I from the RAF. He was religious then, but it was not an attractive religion, God was a

170

forbidding figure who caused fear and guilt in his children. Wilf's religion was of the Law. In fact, if I had been asked to described his idea of God in those days, I would have said that he worshipped a God who didn't love us, but was anxious only to punish us, who suffered our existence, but didn't derive much from the fact that we were alive.

The miracle of his volte-face, from believing in the wrathful God to believing in a God who loves each one of us infinitely, lies behind his great understanding of the Bible and of those who listen to him. For who among us doesn't at times feel unloved, unwanted, inadequate, and a complete failure? It is to those of us who live on the brink of despair (and that includes each one of us at times in our lives) that his words come home. He has stood where they are standing, he knows how it feels – but he knows more than that, in spite of our feelings of hopelessness, we are held within the love of God, the love that the Bible is there to reveal.

PICTURE • PONDER • PRAY • PROMISE

Praise God for the transforming effect of his love in
   human lives.

Pray to God,
   for those whose religion is cramped and judgemental
   those who feel failures and in despair.

A PRAYER

Lord, you have shown your love on Calvary:
Help us to live in simple gratitude and faith. Amen.

The Law was given through Moses:
Grace and truth have come through Jesus Christ.
Let us live in confidence and peace:
In the love of God. Amen.

The second reading is from the foreword by Roy Trevivian to the book *To Me Personally*, by Wilf Wilkinson, 1972, HarperCollins Publishers, London. Reproduced by permission.